PELIC

PELICAN ANTHR
General Edit

MAF

Dr Lucy Mair was born near London and, after taking a degree in classics at Cambridge, joined the staff of the London School of Economics, where she was persuaded by Malinowski to become a social anthropologist. Subsequently she made field studies of village life in Uganda and Nyasaland. Her main interest is in the processes of change which the peoples of the Third World are going through at the present time. She has visited most of the Commonwealth countries in Africa, and has also made a study of recent political developments in New Guinea.

In 1936 she was awarded the Wellcome Medal for an essay on the application of anthropology, and in 1958 she delivered the Lugard Memorial Lecture. From 1963 to 1968 she held the post of Professor of Applied Anthropology at the London School of Economics. Her other books include *An African People in the Twentieth Century*, *Native Policies in Africa*, *Anthropology and Social Change*, *New Nations*, *An Introduction to Social Anthropology*, *Witchcraft*, and *Primitive Government* (available in Pelicans).

LUCY MAIR

MARRIAGE

PENGUIN BOOKS

Penguin Books Ltd, Harmondsworth, Middlesex, England
Penguin Books Inc., 7110 Ambassador Road, Baltimore, Maryland 21207, U.S.A.
Penguin Books Australia Ltd, Ringwood, Victoria, Australia

—

First published 1971

—

Copyright © Lucy Mair, 1971

—

Made and printed in Great Britain by
Cox & Wyman Ltd,
London, Reading and Fakenham
Set in Intertype Baskerville

CONTENTS

CHAPTER I

WHAT IS A HUSBAND FOR?

WHAT is a husband for? To make an honest woman, our grandparents would have said. The phrase epitomizes a number of values, some very widely held, some restricted to particular kinds of society. All are concerned with social rules limiting the circumstances in which children should be begotten, some with limitations on sex relations as such. The word 'honest' is significant; it does not refer to truth-telling or upright business dealing, but to the 'honour' that many peoples cherish, and hold to be tarnished if their womenfolk transgress the sexual rules.

But in this more permissive age and country we may ask in a very different sense, what *is* a husband for? To become a husband limits a man's freedom in many ways, hence one might suppose that there are advantages for somebody else in the rule that the male progenitors of children should be the husbands of their female consorts. The first explanation that comes to hand is a biological one: the human young are helpless for a longer period than those of any other species, the females bearing and suckling them are unfitted to defend them (or themselves) against attack, and must depend upon some man for defence.

But why should this man be the one who begot them? Why should one man be allotted to one brood? Why should not all the males of a group do battle for them together (as, in war, it might be said they sometimes have)?

It is an article of faith with most students of society that one can find everywhere the individual or 'nuclear' family of a man and woman with their children, although this group is sometimes more closely tied to kinsmen outside it than is customary in the industrial world. People began to assert this at a time when some anthropologists believed in 'primitive promiscuity'. They thought that in the early days of humanity there was no restriction on mating and male parenthood was of no account, and that there then developed 'group marriage', in which a number of brothers were supposed to have consorted indiscriminately with a number of sisters and produced offspring who were treated as the communal children of them all. These theories were evolved to account for ways of referring to kin that did not distinguish between one's own father and his brothers, or one's own mother and her sisters. They reflect the nineteenth-century view of marriage as an institution designed primarily to legitimize sex relations, and take no account of its consequences for domestic organization, economic production or the transmission of property.

Modern anthropologists interpret the kin terms that bothered their predecessors in ways that make it unnecessary to assume that there was ever such an institution as group marriage. When they have looked at existing social systems, or at those which have left historical records, they have found none that does not recognize *in some way* a social relationship between male progenitors and their offspring; the qualification 'in some way' is important because of a few striking cases in which there is no domestic family of parents and children. On the other hand, a few societies do not recognize the biological relationship between a woman's mate and her children, but still think they should have a social father.

Nevertheless, the question whether the individual family has existed from man's earliest days has been asked again in the light of the studies that have been made in recent years of the social life of our closest relatives among non-human species, the primates (monkeys and apes). No one existing species is a direct ancestor of man; that is what is meant by references to 'the missing link' between living primates and the earliest known examples of *Homo sapiens*. We can tell from the objects that archaeologists dig up something about the tools that our remote ancestors used, something about the kind of places where they lived, and possibly something about their sources of food. But we can study *behaviour* only by looking at living creatures. So we seem to be debarred for ever from learning what kind of 'ape man' in our family tree first organized his social life on the principle that every female with her young must be placed under the protection of a specified male. This is not because we cannot find primate species organized in that way, but because those that are are not always the closest biologically to *Homo sapiens*. The determining factor seems to be the size of the society, that is the number of animals that move together in search of food and combine for defence. One may find that there is a general responsibility on all the males for the defence of the females and young, who travel in the centre of the group, with the males round them; or that different males in turn look after the offspring of one female. *Some* primates are monogamous and *some* move in bands consisting only of one male and a number of females; among them we can certainly identify a proto-husband. But this 'husband' is concerned more with his sexual rights than with the protection of his offspring.

What of man himself?

In most of the human societies that we know of, mothers and children are dependent on men for more than mere physical protection; indeed in a politically organized society this is not the responsibility of husbands acting as individuals. But existing human societies do not live in caves; their members are never entirely naked; they have some outfit, however small, of material possessions; and they have a division of labour which allots to men, (and denies to women) the production of some of these indispensable goods. Again, why should a woman and her children be expected to get these only from the man who begot the children?

A recent writer on this subject, Robin Fox,[1] starts from the universal biological tie between mother and children and imagines the process by which a husband could 'intrude' into this basic group; or, as he elsewhere puts it, 'father could be

1. Robin Fox, *Kinship and Marriage*, Pelican 1967.

persuaded to stay at home'. There is the possibility that some humans, like some primates, lived in hordes, in which either all the men together protected the women and children or some man, but not necessarily the father, was responsible for each group of mother and children. As the younger generation expected, even after they grew up, to stay with their mothers, brothers and sisters would be always together and a woman's brother would play the role of protector. Both men and women would mate outside the group, and the couples would not live together. Such an arrangement, however, implies that there is a large enough population in continuous contact for mates outside the group of brothers and sisters to be easily found.

If, however, the environment will support only an extremely sparse population, the second generation may have to move away from its predecessors, and the only man available to protect a woman and her children will be the one who fathered the children. But Fox thinks it more likely that where people lived by hunting in small groups, men *wanted* to bring up their sons as good hunters and so were willing to attach themselves permanently to the mothers; and it is certainly true that in many 'primitive' or 'peasant' societies[2] today the status of husband is valued very largely because it gives a man the recognized status of father.

Fox's argument is conjecture. In the last few years some anthropologists have turned their attention to the small nomad populations that still live, as all men once did, by hunting wild animals and gathering wild roots and berries. They certainly recognize marriage, though it is very easy to

2. 'Primitive': a word some people find offensive. Some writers prefer 'tribal', which again some find offensive. 'Primitive' refers to levels of technology. Primitive peoples can be roughly defined as those that have no writing or any form of currency that is valid in transactions of every kind, and expect to gain the greater part of their subsistence directly from their own environment; at the present time there are very few 'untouched primitive' societies. Peasant societies produce goods for market as well as for their own needs; they are incorporated in wider political units, whereas many primitive societies were politically independent until relatively recently.

get married and unmarried. A Hadza woman in Tanzania expects to live in the same camp as her mother, and her husband is expected to supply both these women with meat, which he alone can obtain, since hunting is men's work. But no question arises here of teaching his sons to hunt; the Hadza do not hunt in teams, so numbers are of no importance, and boys learn to hunt from older boys.

Taking examples from the history of an American Indian tribe, the Shoshone, who have been described by Julian Steward, Fox writes of another type of arrangement in which husbands are marginal. The Shoshone, as we first hear of them, practised a little agriculture, though not enough to live on. So the planting and harvesting were left to the women, while the men went hunting. Women lived in scattered homes with their daughters and granddaughters and men looked in on them when they came back from their hunting trips. Then the Shoshone moved to an area where people could live at a greater density, and the men began to share in the work of the fields. Family property was still held to belong to the women, as it had when they were in sole charge of the only durable property, land. By this time property had come to include ritual objects, and since these are usually handled mainly by men they were controlled by brothers of the owners, who lived most of the time with their sisters. When a man married he went to live in his wife's house, but his marriage often did not last very long, and then he returned to his sisters.

By this time we are talking about husbands – particular men whose association with particular women has been formally permitted by society and (usually) recognized in some kind of public ceremony. It is an ideal in all known human societies that the begetting of children should be formally licensed in some way. Yet at the present time there are a number of places where, although this rule is recognized as an ideal, a large proportion of the population disregard it. In such places there is commonly said to be a 'high rate of illegitimacy', and this is often ascribed to the inferior morals and irresponsibility of the people who live there.

Are Husbands necessary?

If it were essential for the protection – in modern times rather for the economic support – of a woman with young children that the father of her children should be legally tied to her, these populations would not be able to survive. But they do. So we come back to the question, what is a husband for?

The populations I am speaking of are neither primitive nor peasant societies. They are the descendants – as we all are – of members of such societies, which in their traditional form made legal marriage a prerequisite for the procreation of children with social approval. They form the lowest strata in highly stratified societies, most of them, though not all, stratified by colour. Those that have been most closely observed are in the Caribbean and in the 'native locations' of African cities. In these places we find women bringing up children, often under great difficulties, as we may learn from the writings of sons whom they have managed to put through school; but they do not fail altogether to bring them up.

This would not be possible if there were no alternative to a husband as the source of support. But there are other possibilities. A woman may bring up her children in her mother's house, and one may find that several generations are linked in this way. The father of her children may give her money even if he does not live with her, or he may build a house for her to live with him even though he does not marry her. Except for a short time when her children are very young, a woman can earn money herself, and where there is much unemployment, and what employment there is is at the lowest level of income, a woman can be as successful a breadwinner as a man.

Yet it would be a mistake to suppose that these populations regard husbands as unnecessary or have evolved a social system that does without marriage. On the contrary, marriage is respected; it is an ideal, but one that many people feel unable to attain. According to Edith Clarke, every Jamaican girl is hoping to find a man 'to be response for me', that is to say, a husband. And every Jamaican mother, when her daughter first gets pregnant, inevitable as she knows this to be, upbraids her, beats her and may turn her out of the house, because her pregnancy has not been sanctioned by a legal marriage. So, they know what husbands are for. First, all husbands are committed in some way to the support of their wives. Even in those societies where it seems to superficial observers that 'the women do all the work', because they hoe the fields and plant the crops, it is commonly the man's responsibility to provide meat, to build and maintain a house, and to clothe his family. In some African societies a woman will leave her husband if he fails to meet these responsibilities.

Husbands, considered as recognized fathers, are most important where they are the source of their children's social status and claims to inheritance. There are societies, to be discussed later in this book, in which descent is traced through the mother (matrilineal), so that a married woman's child belongs to her line as would the child of an unmarried woman. Yet every society of this kind disapproves of the bearing of children without a father whose right to beget them has been legalized by marriage; and the father, in all but a very few cases, has the domestic responsibilities that I have just described.

But in the greater part of the world children take their status from the father; and even where the line of descent is traced through the mother it is usually no disadvantage to have a father of high status. There are societies, about which much will be said in this book, that are divided into *patrilineal* or *agnatic lineages*, groups recruited by descent through males and recognizing common descent as far back as the members can trace their ancestry. A lineage has its patrimony, in land, cattle or capital, and as long as commercial activity is not much developed men depend on inheritance more than on acquisition; where there is commercial activity there is still nothing like inheritance to give you a good start in life. Men are always informally ranked by wealth, and where there is a formal ranking system it is legitimate descent that assigns places in it. Public office is often hereditary; so is the ability to approach non-human beings in ritual to secure their benevolence towards the society or some section of it. Because of the rules that define whom one may or may not marry, status by descent is significant when one is seeking a spouse.

The implications of this aspect of husbandhood and fatherhood are much wider than practical matters of econ-omic support. It is important in two types of society: the equalitarian, and the stratified society in which there is some degree of social mobility. In an equalitarian society, lineage members defend their common property and support one another in seeking redress for injuries. In a society with social mobility, or what is sometimes called the rat-race, a husband/father is expected – and expects – to carry his chil-dren and their mother with him on his upward journey; and an important consideration in the choice of a husband is the question what status their association with him is likely to confer on them.

One can see, then, why husbands are of less significance in the villages of Guyana or the native location of a South African city. The great majority of the men in both these cases can hope for no better fate than to be employed more often than they are unemployed; social mobility is blocked for them in South Africa by laws limiting the occupations they may enter, in Guyana by lack of education and also by a widely accepted feeling that aspiration is vain. For economic support most women must rely in part on their own efforts; many men are not in a position to commit themselves to the total support of a family, and a woman may be able to do as well in petty trade as a man would working for wages. The greatest security comes from owning house-property which can be let, and a woman is as likely to achieve this as a man.

In South Africa regularly contracted marriage is associ-ated either with the traditional values of the rural areas, or with those of a quite different type accepted by the adher-

ents of Christian churches. Among these it is the men who
have had sufficient education to qualify for salaried or professional jobs, as teachers, pastors, clerks and some lawyers
or doctors, who do in fact follow the principles of their
church.

One can also see instances of people who attach value to a
permanent relationship between a man and the mother of
his children, but do not insist that this should be legitimated
by any recognized procedure. The Ngoni of Zambia call a
union entered on without formal preliminaries 'a poorly
fixed marriage', especially if they do not expect it to last; but
if it does last the couple are thought of as husband and wife
just as much as if they had observed all the formalities. John
Barnes[3] explains this by remarking that the formal procedure has lost the significance that it once had. Before they
came under British rule the Ngoni were a people of conquerors who migrated through central Africa, carrying with
them captives from the peoples they defeated and establishing themselves as rulers in the regions where they settled.
Every Ngoni was an aristocrat, and the Ngoni themselves
were elaborately ranked. Sections of the country were placed
under hereditary headmen, and all the agnatic descendants
of an original headman had to live in his area. Hence a man's
position was strictly defined and his status as defined by
legitimate birth was all-important. Ngoni power in Zambia
was destroyed by military defeat in 1898, and there is now
neither advantage nor disadvantage to be derived through
descent. Young couples set up house where they like, near
some kinsman but not necessarily an agnatic kinsman.
Fathers who are anxious to keep their sons near them sometimes perform the legalizing action – here the payment of
bridewealth – many years after they have set up their household, and sometimes even at the moment when the union is
breaking up. But for many this is no longer important.

In some circumstances it is men who want to be fathers
and therefore must be husbands – for it is of the essence of
the argument that the mere act of begetting is rarely enough

3. J. A. Barnes, *Marriage in a Changing Society*, 1951.

to make a man a father in the eyes of society. In others it is
women who want their consorts to become husbands. The
differences can perhaps be roughly correlated with levels of
economic and political development. A man is anxious to be
the head of a numerous household when this provides him
with a large working team; to be a member of a numerous
lineage when this may be necessary for defence. He looks to
his sons for support when he is old or sick. In societies organized in agnatic lineages religion is commonly focused on the
cult of ancestors, and every man wishes to have descendants
to make offerings to his spirit so that he will be commemorated in whatever is considered the appropriate way.
In China up to the Communist revolution it was the first
duty of a son to marry and produce a son to carry on the
ancestor cult. The ancient Romans had very similar ideas. In
lineage-based societies, and indeed in many others, marriage
is an important way of forming alliances; this is one reason
why men wish to become husbands as distinct from fathers.

In societies so organized, then, men wish to marry and
women have no choice. Women do not have difficulty in
inducing their consorts to marry them; but they are often
penalized for entering into unlegalized unions, at any rate if
these produce offspring. It is where the husband is expected
to be the sole economic provider that it is the women who
are most concerned to marry; and, in communities such as
the Guyanese village, marriage is associated with a level of
income that makes this situation possible, and thus with certain social classes in a stratified society. The style of life of a
legally married couple is expected to be what is commonly
described as 'middle-class'. They should have a certain standard of housing and furniture and, even more important, the
husband should be the sole support of the family. Thus it is
only salary-earners with some security who can consider marriage. Moreover, because it is associated with a higher social
class, villagers consider it a kind of pretension to make a
legal marriage; those who are able, and wish, to live at the
standard associated with it usually leave the village and
move to town. In a somewhat similar society, in the Sey-

chelles, it is the actual cost of the wedding, at a standard set by the well-to-do, that makes marriage impossible for some young men in occupations where wages are low; yet couples living *en ménage*, as 'common law unions' are called there, are nowhere in the majority.

Sometimes a couple who have lived a long time in a common law union decide to marry, and this at once changes both their legal relationship and their mutual expectations. In Guyana the ideal is that the wife should have a servant girl, and so no longer do all the household work, let alone contribute to the family income. And there may be subtler touches. To move to another part of the world, the charming story from Sierra Leone by Abioseh Nicol, *The Truly Married Wife*, finishes with the lady, the day after the wedding, telling her husband that it is now for *him* to make the morning tea. But the woman surrenders independence not only in the sense that she is relieved of hard work and economic responsibility. Her husband is bound to her, but so is she to him. In London, as well as in more exotic places, women separated by death or divorce from an unsatisfactory husband often prefer to make a new union without legal marriage and the rights it gives the husband.

These examples do not show that there is any society which dispenses with marriage; on the contrary. We know of no society in the contemporary or recorded world which does not recognize it – indeed there are many anthropologists who will not consider the possibility that there might have been human societies which did not recognize the role of husband–father. But by approaching the subject through instances where the legal institution of marriage is, or might be, lacking, I hope I have thrown some light on its social significance, something which is generally taken for granted. One conclusion to which these instances point is that husbands are important mainly as fathers; that is to say, as men who give their name, their status in so far as this is inherited, and the right to inherit their property, to the children of a woman with whom they have made a particular kind of contract.

CHAPTER 2

WHOM MAY ONE MARRY?

MARRIAGE in societies where a person's prospects in life depend primarily on his status by birth and on that of the people to whom he is allied by kinship or affinity has a very different significance from that which industrialized societies attach to it. In the latter societies we worry about the compatibility of spouses, and the degree of incompatibility that should be considered sufficient to justify their separation. Except for those who hold religious convictions in relation to marriage vows, the prime consideration in such discussions is the welfare of the children of unsuccessful marriages, whose emotional life, we have learned in recent years, may be blighted by the dissensions of their parents. In these societies a person makes his own way in a profession or employment; many people are handicapped by the class they are born into, but only a few gain or lose by the individual status of their parents. To be married is by no means indispensable, since the domestic labour that was once supplied by wives is now provided by machines, and the economic support that once came from husbands can now be provided by a woman's own earnings. Many women do not wish to bear children, and there are only a few who find in this the sole reason for existence.

In societies based on a subsistence economy all this is different. There is no wage-labour, and the production of food is the work of kin groups organized as teams. It is expected that everyone should marry as soon as possible; how soon this will be in different societies is a question to be considered later. Women are expected, and expect, to bear as many children as they can. Marriage is a matter of the allocation of women to husbands, sometimes, but not always, taking individual choice into consideration. Personal compatibility is not a matter for much concern; spouses spend little time together in any case. Marriage is primarily of importance as a knot in the network of kinship links that bind such a society together. It is the formally recognized means of recruiting new members to a line of descent, and it creates alliances between such lines. The making of marriages depends in part on the claims that men are entitled to make on one another's daughters; in part on the kind of alliance that men, seeking wives for themselves or their sons, believe will be advantageous; and to a small degree, and more in some societies than in others, on the individual preferences of a man and a woman. Marriage is a matter of serious concern to a much larger number of people than the spouses themselves. Hence it is hedged about with rules and ceremonies to a much greater extent than it is in those societies, which Radcliffe-Brown long ago reminded us are exceptional, that make an ideal of 'marriage for love'.

Anyone who thinks it is shocking to regard marriage in this matter-of-fact, even calculating, way had better not read this book. For those who are willing to continue, the next step is to ask what rules prohibit, and what rules seek to enforce, marriage between persons related in specified ways.

It can be taken as a characteristic of the human race, which distinguishes them from many other animals, that siblings do not mate with siblings, nor parents with children. The breach of this rule, which does sometimes happen, is called incest. It is obvious that persons between whom mating is forbidden cannot marry. But the rules that limit the choice of spouses rule out many more persons than this principle would forbid; and the prohibitions are not necessarily concerned to prevent the mating of close kin.

The French anthropologist Lévi-Strauss maintains that the crucial distinction between humans and other animals lies in the prohibition of incest. This, he says, marks the transition from the realm of nature, in which most actions are instinctive — fixed responses to a limited number of stimuli — to that of culture, in which the right behaviour in given situations is explicitly taught to the younger generation by their elders. Two characteristics peculiar to man make this possible: that men communicate in verbal language, and that the young of the human species take longer to grow to maturity than those of any other. During the long period of childhood they are 'socialized', to use the hideous word invented by sociologists, or 'enculturated', to use the equally hideous word invented by an American anthropologist, with the effect that most adults take for granted the rules of conduct of the society to which they belong. Not all do; and this is what makes the study of human society so much more interesting to most people than that of other social animals.

Part of this process consists in inculcating the rule against incest. Some societies regard this as a peculiarly horrible sin; in some, such as Victorian and Edwardian England, it has been too horrible to mention, so that the well brought up grew up without even hearing about it. Others, such as the Tallensi in Northern Ghana, find the idea of incest unthinkable simply because to them it is absurd. The sexual permissiveness of the contemporary western world has not done away with this restriction.

For Lévi-Strauss and his followers, what differentiates humans from other animals is not that they have social life, for many animals do, but that the basis of their life lies in reciprocal exchange. Language is one form of exchange. More tangible forms are the exchange of goods and of women. If siblings may not mate, the exchange of women becomes necessary for the continuation of the society; and Lévi-Strauss comes near to arguing that incest was forbidden in order to force men to exchange their sisters. He does go as far as to say that marriage rules which result in the exchange of women between groups must have been expressly devised by the leading minds of primitive societies. Well, perhaps they were; no one can say.

Just before Lévi-Strauss published the first edition of his *Structures elémentáires de la parenté* in 1949,[1] an American

---

1. The second edition has been translated into English with the title *Elementary Structures of Kinship*.

anthropologist, Leslie A. White, put forward a somewhat similar but less abstract explanation of the prohibition. He took as his starting-point the division of labour within the family, and argued that as soon as people became aware of the advantages of cooperation with an elementary specialization of tasks, they would unconsciously recognize that a wider field of cooperation had even greater advantages; in order to achieve it they would begin to make marriages outside the family and would come to forbid marriage within it.

Both these writers, eminent as they are, treat *incest*, which is a matter of *mating*, as if it were synonymous with *exogamy*, which is a matter of *marriage*. But both reject the idea that the prohibition of incest is the expression of an 'instinctive' repugnance to the idea of mating with close kin, which supposedly springs from an 'instinctive' recognition that this is biologically dangerous; and if we abandon this idea it becomes easier, or at least less difficult, to account for the exceptional cases where the marriage of siblings has been permitted.

Although it is common, it is not universal for people to be taught to regard incest with horror. In many societies it is thought of as a sin which divine beings will automatically punish; but in others, such as modern Britain, it is punished by the law, yet not very severely. Various theories have been advanced to explain the horror; they are described in Robin Fox's *Kinship and Marriage*. When, however, Fox discusses marriage he simply takes it as given that humans do not marry within the family, and develops the argument from there; this is what I shall do from now on.

Marriage as an Exchange

Lévi-Strauss' theory rests on the axiom that, in any society, it is men who dispose of women in marriage and not *vice versa*. A glance at the marriage service in the Book of Common Prayer is enough to remind us how universal is this rule. The 'giving away' of the bride, though it has lost its

meaning, is still an indispensable part of the church ceremony; and it is not so long since the question 'Who giveth
this woman to be married to this man?' referred to some
male guardian without whose consent the marriage could
not be made. Lévi-Strauss, who is more interested in under-
lying principles than in everyday life, tends to assimilate
women to property. Certainly there are analogies to be
drawn between different types of exchange; but the notion
still cherished by earnest feminists, that in some societies
today the status of a wife is identical with that of a slave, is
mistaken, as later chapters will show.

Fox has made an imaginative reconstruction of the life of
the first humans. Although it is speculative, it goes beyond
generalizations to concrete possibilities, and is worth considering. The picture he draws is of an environment so poor
in resources that individual families had to live some distance apart. They would join with others from time to time,
perhaps for some type of hunting that needed larger
numbers, or for ritual, a specifically human activity which
could be brought into the category of exchange if one
thought of it as a transaction between men and gods.
Through these meetings the young men, or their elders on
their behalf, would find their mates.

Fox then envisages some kind of tacit agreement between
two bands to exchange their sisters and daughters. If there
happened to be in each band a brother and sister of marriageable age there could be a direct exchange, and this is an
arrangement that some peoples, for example the Tiv of
Northern Nigeria, still regard as the ideal. But in a hard
environment where many children die in infancy this might
not always be practicable; the exchange might not be made
immediately, and the incoming woman might not be the
sister of the man who received a wife but someone less
closely related.

A pact for the exchange of women between two groups
imposes narrow limitations on the choice of marriage partner; indeed, this is the reason why the British in Nigeria
refused to countenance exchange marriage among the Tiv.

The subject of what is called 'prescriptive' and 'preferential' marriage will be discussed later, but it is clearly interwoven with the rules forbidding marriage between certain categories of persons; it is to these that I now return.

Exogamy

The rule that one must find one's marriage partner *outside* a defined group is called *exogamy* (marrying outside); the rule that one must find her *within* a defined group is *endogamy* (marrying inside). These two useful words were coined by J. F. McLennan, one of the fathers of British anthropology.

In many societies of simple technology descent is traced *unilineally*; that is to say, *either* through males *or* through females. A descent group united by this principle, if the members can trace their genealogy, is called a *lineage*. Lineages may be organized into clans, the members of which have a common name and assume that this is evidence of common ancestry. Lineages are generally exogamous, and the prohibition of intermarriage commonly extends to fellow clansmen; the name is enough to indicate whether a given person is a permitted partner.

In addition to the rule of lineage exogamy there are often prohibitions against marriage with kin on the side of the parent from whom one does not take one's lineage membership. The effect of these is to rule out marriage with people who have any common ancestor for a small number of generations back, and the two types of prohibition taken together have the consequence that a man seeking a wife must usually go outside, even if not very far outside, the small community in which he has grown up.

Exogamous marriage directly links lineages, and thus also links village groups; and since it is a relationship implying amity not only between the spouses but between their kin, it has clear political significance. In turbulent societies it extends the area within which an individual can count on a peaceful reception; in those in which order is more effectively enforced, marriage alliances can be utilized in the pursuit of wealth, power or preferment. Tylor, conjecturing on the possible origin of exogamy, said that for primitive man it was a choice between 'marrying out or being killed out'. It might be rash to picture the elders of the hunting band putting their heads together and coming to this conclusion; but both the history of past centuries and the observation of small-scale societies today show how keenly the parents of nubile children have, as individuals, appreciated the significance of marriage as an alliance. Limitations on the marriage of near kin result in the constant making of new alliances; but equally they prevent the renewal of old ones.

Marriage of Close Kin

An important exception to the rule of lineage exogamy is provided by a number of Arab tribes, and by some other nomadic herdsmen who are organized in a similar way. Nomad Arabs attach great importance to the principle of patrilineal descent. Each tribe regards itself as one vast lineage divided into segments founded by the sons, grandsons and so on of the first ancestor, and each section of a tribe is called by the name of its putative founder. The group which migrates and camps together is conceived to be a lineage, and the living men are divided into sections known as 'the children of' their father or grandfather. The leadership of such a group descends in the paternal line. When they camp the tents are pitched in an order which represents the closeness or distance of agnatic kinship between the heads of houses – sons near their fathers, first cousins further apart, and so on. When marriages are to be arranged or stock disposed of it is the adult males of the smallest recognized lineage – 'the children of Hussein' or whoever it may be – who consult together.

Yet they not only permit but expect marriages to be made within the lineage, and between the closest possible kin (outside the family of parents and children, of course). If two brothers have a son and daughter of marriageable age – or even infant children who may be betrothed ahead of time – they should marry; the boy's father has a right to claim the girl for his son, and more distantly related or unrelated suitors should make sure that nobody has such a claim before they offer themselves.

Where this is the rule, the links of agnatic descent are reinforced by those of marriage, and the tendency of lineages to divide as the generations succeed one another is checked. This system is credited with just the same advantages, as a source of security, as are ascribed to lineage exogamy, which forces people to make new alliances in each generation. For the Bedouin in Israel the rule is said to be especially important among those tribes which have peasants settled on their land, as it concentrates together a small number of men who might have to combine their forces against a rebellion. The number of men in an autonomous section of a Bedouin tribe is in any case small, but it would be even smaller if the sections were constantly splitting. Where a tribe has not a subject peasant population people are more inclined to form marriage alliances outside the lineage. The members of a settled Arab community in Israel themselves explained the preference for marriage within the lineage by the necessity of keeping the kin group together in case of strife with neighbours.[2] In so far, then, as marriage cements alliances, it would seem that to the Arabs it is more important to reinforce the solidarity of close kin than to establish friendly relationships with other groups.

Another Arab people, the Baggara of the Sudan, gave reasons for the rule that belong rather to the field of relations within the family. Women say a child is better cared for if its mother is in her own home among her sisters, who can help her in crises such as sickness; men say that if their sisters go away to marry, the children grow up among their enemies and are themselves brought up as enemies – a contrast to the attitude of people for whom marriage links create friends in a field of potential enemies. A more hard-headed reason is to

2. A. Cohen, *Arab Border Villages in Israel,* 1965, p. 119.

be found in the property system, which influences the nature of marriage in many ways. Baggara women, unlike many others, have their own property in cattle, but like most others they have to leave the care and disposal of their property to their brothers. If a woman leaves her lineage camp to marry elsewhere, her cattle are left behind, and are no use to her husband; so men prefer to marry women whose cattle they can use. Yet – and this is interesting – they do have a feeling that there is something anomalous in marrying women whom they call sister,[3] since, like most peoples who are organized in lineages, they use the same word for sisters and cousins.

The reason given by the Norwegian anthropologist, F. Barth, for the permission of the marriage of patrilineal cousins among the Nomad Basseri of Southern Persia is again the prevention of divisions within the group.[4] Like the Arabs, they believe their tribe to be one vast lineage, into a section of which everybody fits; but here the groups that camp together are not lineages at all but collections of households linked by kinship in various ways. Men inherit their fathers' herds, but since each man receives his share at marriage there is no continuing lineage estate. A woman's guardian, who arranges her marriage, is her own father or brother. Although there is a recognized camp leader, he has no coercive power, so if he wants to hold the group together and prevent sections moving off whenever they have their own ideas about where to find the best grazing, he must build up influence by marriage links. This is a reason for leaders and aspirants to leadership to marry their daughters to men within the camp in preference to outsiders. But in this case marriages with agnatic cousins are a small proportion of the whole.

Exceptionally among Bantu, the Tswana, although they reckon descent in the male line, also permit marriage between close agnates, and the genealogies collected by Schapera show that this was often practised, particularly among

3. I. G. Cunnison, *Baggara Arabs*, 1966, pp. 90–94.
4. F. Barth, *Nomads of South Persia*, 1964.

'royals' (chiefs and men descended from chiefs). The royal lines of the kingdoms of the interior of West Africa also make such marriages.

Schapera's explanation[5] resembles one of those given by the Arabs, namely that marriages within the lineage prevent its dispersion. In this case, however, it is not a question of keeping the lineage together on the ground. Members of chiefs' families are made headmen of wards – sections of territory – and so dispersed over the chiefdom. Each has his following of commoners and so may be tempted to secede, or to try to make himself chief. Within the wards brothers may be rivals for the headmanship. In such contests men expect the backing of maternal kin who, since they are not members of the same lineage, cannot compete with them, and who in principle are expected to support their sisters' children. By marrying the sister of a potential rival one converts him into a maternal relative for one's children.

There have been societies in which even the marriage of full brothers and sisters was permitted. A few years ago an anthropologist referred to, without specifying them, a considerable number of reports from different parts of the world which alleged this and which he had been able to investigate.[6] For the present, however, we have to be satisfied with the text-book cases of Egypt, the kings of Hawaii and the Incas of Peru. Only in Egypt in Roman times is it established that such marriages were generally permitted; in Hawaii and Peru they were confined to the families of princes. One of the arguments for brother–sister marriage in Egypt closely resembles one of those for the intra-lineage marriages of the Arabs; women inherited property in their own right and so the marriage of brother and sister kept the patrimony together. Such marriages were commoner in cities, where one would expect to find the wealthier people.

5. I. Schapera, 'Marriage of Near Kin among the Tswana', *Africa*, 1957, pp. 139–59.
6. R. Middleton, 'Brother–Sister and Father–Daughter Marriage in Ancient Egypt', *American Sociological Review*, 1962, p. 611.

Of the Hawaiian kings and the Incas it is generally said that they married their sisters in order to maintain the purity of the royal blood and the uniqueness of the ruling line. This has also been said of the Pharaohs, though the records show that they did not *always* marry their sisters or even other women of royal descent, and that the sons even of slave-women sometimes succeeded their fathers. It has also been argued that brother–sister marriage reduced the number of lines that might compete for the succession. But one king is on record as saying that, as he had only two children, it would be dangerous to limit the number of successors by marrying them together; he would rather marry each into the family of a high-ranking commoner.[7]

As was noted earlier, the restrictions on marriage implied in the word exogamy – that the partner must be found outside the lineage – are usually complemented by prohibitions on marriage with a narrower range of kin related through the non-lineage parent; and where people are not organized in lineages, but give equal weight to kin traced through both parents, there will be rules forbidding marriage between persons who have a common ancestor within a defined number of generations. One never finds it stated as a rule that a territorial group, such as a village, must be exogamous, but often the effect of the range of prohibitions is that the spouse must be found outside the village, or this will simply be thought preferable, even though a permitted partner could be found inside it. But there is no generalization without exception. There are circumstances in which marriage within the village is preferred; we shall come to these later.

Endogamy

Are lineages which are not exogamous necessarily endogamous? No, they permit marriages which could be called endogamous, but endogamy strictly means a rule that one *must* marry within a defined group and may not go outside it

7. Middleton, op. cit., pp. 609ff.

for a partner. Note that I refer to a rule; most rules are sometimes broken, and there are often ways of condoning a breach. Nevertheless, the theory of every endogamous group is that its exclusiveness is preserved by forbidding the introduction of marriage partners from outside. Within endogamous groups there are, of course, prohibitions on marriage within a certain range of kin, and Indians and Chinese often prefer also to find marriage partners outside their home village, though this is practical rather than jural exogamy. One finds endogamy in societies that are complex enough to include within one political and economic system communities with differing ways of life which they, or at least the dominant section, wish to keep distinct. The emphasis here is not on binding those inside more closely together but on maintaining a boundary against outsiders. Endogamy goes with social stratification, but stratified societies are not necessarily divided into endogamous groups. In any society people tend to marry within a limited circle, whether the limitations are geographical, as they are when people can only travel on foot, or of a less tangible nature. Where there are wide differences in income or education, and especially where these are associated with differences in the way people organize their everyday life, those who are most alike are inevitably most closely associated; and after all, people must choose their marriage partners among their acquaintances. Sometimes parents disapprove, and often there are social difficulties, when people from different classes marry; John Osborne's *Look Back in Anger* put this on record. But one should not talk of endogamy unless there is an explicit rule, and either this *cannot* be broken, because a union which broke it would not be regarded as legal, or there are recognized formal procedures for dealing with a breach.

The classic example of endogamy is the Hindu caste system; so much so that the term caste is sometimes applied to quasi-endogamous divisions of societies very differently organized from those of India. The Indian system is bound up with the idea of ritual purity, in the negative form of avoidance of the pollution incurred in handling unclean substances. Some occupations are in their nature polluting; tanners handle the hides of dead cattle, distillers make strong drink which strict Hindus should not touch, washermen and sweepers are in contact with dirt. Castes are called by the names of occupations and are ranked according to the degree of cleanness or uncleanness associated with each. All members of a caste do not necessarily follow the caste occupation. But this does not make any difference to their ranking. Caste membership is hereditary, as membership of any endogamous group must naturally be.

Marriage outside the caste is forbidden;[8] that is to say, a union between members of different castes cannot be legalized, since to make a marriage legal the kin of both partners must take part in rituals performed by an appropriate specialist, and none of these people would lend their countenance to an inter-caste marriage. Nevertheless, people sometimes enter into unlegalized unions, and, when they do, usually have children. The caste status of the children must then be determined, and this will be important principally when the time comes for them to marry. They may find that only people of similar mixed parentage will accept them as partners. But if the parents are of castes not too widely separated in the hierarchy, and the father is a respected man, the breach will be forgotten and the children recognized as members of their father's caste. When marriages are being arranged, the memory of an irregular union in one partner's ancestry is considered a disqualification, but on the man's side it may be ignored if his family are wealthy enough.

The study made by E. R. Leach of the small village of Pul Eliya in Ceylon[9] led him to a somewhat similar conclusion about attitudes towards endogamy. Here marriage need not be accompanied by the same formalities as in India; a couple who set up house together are automatically regarded as married. Hence it is quite possible for a marriage to be made which breaks the rule of endogamy. Then someone is likely

8. With an important exception which is discussed in Chapter 5.
9. E. R. Leach, *Pul Eliya*, 1961.

to bring the matter before the court of the sub-caste, which deals with such cases. Theoretically every breach of the rule is a sin committed by the woman, which brings pollution and hence potential disaster upon the entire village. But there are two possible reactions to this. Either the couple, and possibly the woman's kinsmen, may be expelled from the village, or the offending man may pay a fine and be forgiven. In effect, as Leach remarks, he buys his way into the sub-caste. Theories of pollution are forgotten if he is a desirable village member; they are invoked if somebody would like his property and he has no influential backers.

In Africa there was, until a few years ago, a cluster of kingdoms known as the Interlacustrine Bantu states on the high ground between Lake Victoria and the western arm of the Great Rift Valley. They are no longer kingdoms, because in Uganda a government which drew its support from other parts of the country deposed the kings in 1966, and in Ruanda the king was thrown out by a popular revolution. But for three hundred years they had been kingdoms in which cattle-owning invaders from the north dominated an older population of cultivators. The extent to which the cattle people sought to maintain their distinct identity differed from one to another. In Buganda, which is lower-lying and not suitable for cattle, distinctions disappeared altogether. It was in Ankole and Ruanda that they were most insisted upon. Here, as among most of the cattle-owning peoples of Africa, marriage is legalized by the transfer of cattle from the husband's lineage to the wife's. According to Oberg's[10] account of Ankole the agricultural lower class were not allowed to own cattle, so that it was formally impossible for the pastoralists to marry them. But in Ruanda as described by Maquet,[11] although the ruling Tutsi emphasized to an extreme degree their distinctiveness from the Hutu cultivators, there was no rule of endogamy. A poor Tutsi man could marry a Hutu girl, for whom he would give fewer

10. K. Oberg, 'The Kingdom of Ankole in Uganda', in *African Political Systems*, ed. Fortes and Evans-Pritchard, 1940.

11. J. J. Maquet, *The Premise of Inequality in Uganda*, 1961.

cattle, and a prosperous Hutu could marry a Tutsi girl, also a Tutsi might give a daughter to a Hutu dependent.

Where the rule of endogamy and the marriage procedures make it actually impossible for a marriage to be made outside the group, the effect of a breach of the rule is to produce children of indeterminate status. If, as in India or Ceylon, there are large numbers of endogamous groups, their situation will depend on the special factors in each case. If, as in Ankole, there are only two, the offspring of miscegenation, as it is called when people believe their society to be made up of different races, are apt to be placed in a single category and given a name. In English we speak of 'half-caste' although we do not recognize divisions into caste. But since 'caste' originally meant 'race' perhaps there is a logical justification for the usage.

One must say, then, of the rule of endogamy that it is very much harder to enforce than that of exogamy. Its benefits lie in the maintenance of group solidarity rather than in any advantage to individual members, whereas exogamy is no hindrance to the pursuit of individual advantage by making useful alliances. There are few, if any, groups of which one could say that they not only profess to be, but are, endogamous in the sense of mating, as well as marrying, only within the group.

Nevertheless, attempts to maintain group endogamy can be found in the large-scale societies of the industrial world as well as in those of simple technology with which this book is mainly concerned. Such groups are commonly united by religious belief, and seek by rules against marriage outside to protect their membership from attrition.

Jewish endogamy has its roots in the distant past when the Jews were a pastoral people of the Middle East, committed to maintaining their distinct identity as God's chosen people. For orthodox adherents to Judaism it is still the rule today. Just as in biblical times, marriage outside the group is conceived in terms of the introduction of alien wives; the essential qualification for membership of a Jewish community is to have a Jewish mother. In the days when we first read of

God's anger at a breach of the rule, it was the sons of Israel who 'took to themselves wives' from the neighbouring peoples; in those days women could not choose their husbands. The Jewish marriage ritual would not be performed for a marriage with non-Jews. In the past the family of a Jew who made such a marriage would hold a funeral ceremony for him, and even today, if asked about such a man, they sometimes speak of him as if he were dead or had never existed. But although his action would once have been described as 'the most heinous crime that could be committed short of conversion to Christianity', and as late as 1958 was officially said to be a violation of one of the most important of all Jewish prohibitions, it is not now penalized, except in so far as he is debarred from holding a position of religious leadership. Endogamy for Jews is now more commonly interpreted to mean that marriage is forbidden with a person not of the Jewish religion; that is, the rule is now a matter of beliefs rather than of descent.

Religious communities which wish to extend their membership cannot, like the Indian castes, make it depend on birth. Therefore persons born in the faith may marry converts; it is marriage with the adherents of other beliefs or of none that is disapproved.

The largest and most conspicuous endogamous group of this kind is the Roman Catholic Church. The essence of its disapproval – which in its contemporary form falls somewhat short of a prohibition – is its fear that the community will be eroded if the next generation grows up under other than Catholic influences. The Church has sometimes accepted an undertaking that the children of a marriage with a non-Catholic will be brought up in the Catholic faith.

But both Jews and Catholics live today in societies where one can contract a marriage before an official who is not concerned with ritual; today neither priests nor parents can exercise an effective veto on marriage choices.

The most rigorously endogamous religious communities in England today are very small sects whose beliefs entail the rejection of many of the social activities of the wider society (such as playing cards, dancing or perhaps even music), or even, as far as possible, insulation from contact with non-members. Where the latter rule is followed, as it is by the more extreme sects of the Plymouth Brethren, the group must obviously be endogamous, and it is reported of one of these, the Exclusive Brethren, that the network of kin ties which links their members as the result of this rule makes them more united with their fellow members anywhere in Britain than they are with their nearest neighbours.

There is one example in the industrialized world of what might well be described as caste endogamy, though the rule is not supported by the elaborate concepts of pollution on which the caste system rests in India. This is the Republic of South Africa, most of the white population of which are committed to the maintenance of the purity of their descent, or, to put it more realistically, to the prevention of further intermixture with peoples of African or Asian ancestry. The South African *apartheid* policy not only allocates separate areas of residence and separate occupations to members of different 'races', but makes it a criminal offence for persons assigned to different 'racial' categories to have sex relations, and legally impossible for them to marry. A couple who make a forbidden marriage outside South Africa may not live together if they return there; and a couple who have supposed themselves to be legally married may be separated if the authorities decide that one has been wrongly classified. Here we are again squarely in the field where the maintenance of a dominant group is supported by a theory of the need to preserve purity of the 'blood'.

CHAPTER 3

WHOM MUST ONE MARRY?

ANTHROPOLOGISTS generally agree that there is no society which does not prohibit the marriage of people related in specified degrees of kinship. There is rather more disagreement over the question whether any societies insist that persons related in a particular way must marry. There are many in which it is considered that the ideal marriage is one between cousins, a fact sufficient to disprove any theory that rules of exogamy arise from some 'instinctive' recognition of the supposedly deleterious consequences of mating with close kin. A rule that cousins must marry is called *prescriptive*; where there is merely a general consensus in favour this is called *preferential* marriage. It will be clear that among small populations the effect of restrictions on marriage into specific descent lines may be to leave only one available, so that prohibition and preference are two sides of a penny.

The previous chapter mentioned that exogamy was explained by Lévi-Strauss as a rule making necessary the exchange of women, which he regards as one of the basic forms of human communication. Indeed he seems to regard the giving of sisters as more important than the taking of wives, and even to argue that children are produced simply so that the exchange can continue through the generations. His massive book on kinship, *Les Structures elémentaires de la parenté*, begins by saying that he is examining systems which prescribe marriage with a certain category of kin, and he appears to argue that prescriptive marriage rules are characteristic of the simplest and preferential rules of more complex social structures. But after some heated controversy in which the Oxford anthropologist, Rodney Needham, maintained that critics of Lévi-Strauss had confused the prescriptive with the preferential, he himself said in a lecture in London that he saw no difference between the two. 'Even a preferential system', he said, 'is prescriptive at the level of the model, while even a prescriptive system cannot but be preferential at the level of reality.' This would certainly seem like commonsense. On the one hand, people very frequently claim that there is a rule prescribing whatever they think should be done; on the other, it is difficult to imagine a society in which a mate in the particular genealogical relationship would *always* be available when the time came to arrange a marriage, and we now have field records from some societies showing numbers of cases where there was no appropriate partner. Supposedly prescriptive systems may work out quite differently from what the rules appear to require; and where the rules have been described as preferential one may find that only a third of marriages are of the type supposedly preferred. So the question that heads this chapter is really a bogus one.

Cross-cousin Marriage

Before going further we should make it clear what kind of cousin people are expected to marry. In a lineage system some cousins will be lineage mates and so debarred from marrying (unless they are Arabs, as the previous chapter indicated). These must be the ones who derive their cousinship from parents of the same sex – two brothers or two sisters. Persons so related are called parallel cousins, and are of little importance in the present context. Those we are here concerned with are the children of a brother and a sister, and they are technically called cross-cousins. Such a pair *cannot* be lineage mates, since lineage membership is derived from *either* mother *or* father, and so they are never debarred from marriage by lineage exogamy.

One may have cross-cousins on either side of the family, children of one's father's sister or of one's mother's brother. When cross-cousins marry, if the man marries his mother's brother's daughter, the woman marries her father's sister's son. So, in order to avoid inextricable confusion, we describe the alternative forms of cross-cousin marriage from the point of view of the man. Marriage with the mother's brother's daughter is, then, *matrilateral,* and that with father's sister's daughter *patrilateral,* cross-cousin marriage. The former is by far the more common.

For fifty years or so anthropologists worried over the question why people thought it was so important to marry their cousins. The fact that they did so had come to notice when field-workers were collecting genealogies in Oceania by a technique which enables one at the same time to ask what names people give to different categories of kin. To do this you must put the person questioned in the middle of the picture and consider everyone else in terms of their relationship to him; and he may well say 'I call all these women by the same term because I ought to marry one of them'. This presents cross-cousin marriage as a rule applying to individuals.

According to Nur Yalman, the rule among the Kandyan Sinhalese, who are not organized in lineages, is in fact one for individuals. Property, which in all peasant societies consists mainly in land, is inherited and transmitted by both men and women. When a woman marries she may either ask for her share of the parental land, or leave it with her parents, from whom it passes to her brothers. When her children grow up she can assert her claim by arranging marriages with her brother's children. (But it seems from his account to be brothers and not sisters who actually assert claims.)

But if we turn from the individual to the lineage it can be argued, as Lévi-Strauss argues, that what for an individual is the right to marry his cousin, for the lineage as a group is part of a system for the exchange of women. To Lévi-Strauss this is a way of expressing the inherent need for communication. Robin Fox in his imaginary picture of the first men (or some of them) argues instead that given the prohibition against mating within the family, which he takes as axiomatic, isolated family groups could not continue to exist.

They must have found mates outside on those occasions when a number of people came together for some special purpose, and two groups could have come to a kind of pact to intermarry through the generations. If there are only two such groups in the social universe, then a man's mother's brother's daughter must *also* be his father's sister's daughter. This is called *double* cross-cousin marriage. But of course it does not spring from a rule that a man in search of a wife must look for a double cross-cousin; it is the inevitable consequence of the exchange system.

It should not be supposed that men are always expected to marry their *first* cousins; I have remarked that such a rule would be impossibly difficult. What is expected of them in an exchange system is to find their wives in the lineage into which their sisters have married. All these women will be cousins of a sort, though the cousinship may be pretty distant after the exchange has been going on for some generations.

This system of reciprocal exchange is called Kariera type marriage after the Australian aborigines who practise it. The whole tribe is conceived as belonging to two exogamous sections, which are technically known as *moieties* (the word only means 'half'). Each moiety includes a number of lineages, and lineages in opposing moieties may be paired for marriage purposes.

But although the Kariera have given their name to a type, it is not from them that we learn the kind of difficulty that a rule of exchange creates or what people do to get round it. For this we must look to the Tiv of the Benue Valley in Nigeria, among whom two anthropologists worked in 1949–50.

Marriage by Exchange

The Tiv regard the ideal marriage as one in which two men simultaneously exchange sisters. In 1927 the British government declared this form of marriage illegal, holding, quite correctly, that it severely limited the freedom of choice of the woman given in exchange. They said, indeed, that it was tantamount to slavery, which they were committed to abolish. In this they exaggerated somewhat; Tiv had always recognized other ways of getting a wife, notably by the payment of bridewealth, but these were considered inferior. So Paul and Laura Bohannan were not able actually to follow the procedure for the arrangement of a marriage exchange, but they could talk to plenty of people who had been married that way.

The rule was that every woman had a 'marriage guardian' who had the right to decide whom she should marry, and who received, and disposed of to some marriageable youth, the woman who came in in exchange for her. The same men now receive bridewealth payments and dispose of them in making new marriages. Individual women were allotted to different brothers as guardians, so that there were numbers of marriage guardians, not agnatic groups with a single head who decided all marriages. But marriage guardians did of course form agnatic groups which were exogamous. Such a group might be only the sons of one father, or it might be a lineage with a common ancestor some generations back. Of course they consulted together when decisions had to be taken.

It was recognized that it was very seldom possible to make two marriages within a few months. A girl of marriageable age might not be available, or if she was there might be no young man seeking a wife. So the exchange would have to be postponed, perhaps for a whole generation. When a woman was received in return for an earlier marriage, if there was nobody to marry her to, the man to whom she was given might hand her on to pay some long-standing debt of his own. One case was remembered where a girl passed through the wardship of five men and was eventually married in a village a hundred miles from her home. This must have been a hard experience for her; but when she was eventually married she would not be, or be treated like, a slave.

As late as 1967 a system of this kind was found to be still in operation among the Nyende in the north-west of Dahomey. Huber, the Swiss anthropologist who worked there, recorded cases which show how the problem of unequal numbers of brothers and sisters in individual families may be dealt with. A man who has no sister – or whose sister has been exchanged for a second wife by his father – will go to a brother of his father for a daughter to exchange. This may leave a younger brother of this girl, not at that time old enough to marry, with no sister for himself. He may ask for the right to give in exchange for his wife a daughter of the cousin who gave away his elder sister. Thus debts arise within lineages as well as between them. It is common for Nyende women to elope very soon after their marriage with a lover whom they prefer to the designated husband; the latter can then demand another woman or take back the one he gave in exchange. Nyende say this used not to happen in the old days; certainly elopement is easier now that the couple can leave their own country for some place of employment. Like the Tiv, the Nyende recognize an alternative way of legalizing marriage by the transfer of goods.[1]

In these examples, the whole population who call themselves Tiv or Nyende are not divided into exchanging moieties, and in real life we are much more likely to find exchanging partnerships between small sections of the total society than a complicated all-embracing system. One should mention, however, another Australian system that is quoted in textbooks as typical – the Aranda. The Aranda hold that a first cousin is 'too close', though they also hold that descent groups should exchange women. Whereas the Kariera expect a man to find his wife where his father did – that is, in his mother's lineage – the Aranda think he should skip a generation and take his wife from the lineage of his grandmother (his father's mother). Father and son are thus linked by exchange with different lineages. For such a system there must be at least four exchanging divisions.

Much of the information that has been used as a basis for explanations and theories of Australian marriage rules consists of statements by informants of what *ought* to be done.

1. H. Huber, 'Le Principe de la reciprocité dans le mariage Nyende', *Africa* 1969, pp. 260–74.

Most of the anthropologists of more recent days have found that it is necessary to compare these with observations and records of actual cases, and these have always revealed that what ought to be done is very often not done. In the Australian case close study has revealed that the rule of cross-cousin marriage has two aspects. In one it simply means, as was said before, that a man should find his wife in a particular lineage, and in this sense, among the Gidjingali studied by Hiatt, nine-tenths of marriages conformed to the rule. But when first cousins are concerned the situation is not so much that a man *must* marry his cousin but that he has a right to marry her; the rule might be better stated in the form that a woman must marry a cousin if there is one who wants her. Bear in mind that we are considering a world in which parents dispose of their daughters, and that in very sparse populations, where polygyny is permitted, a claim to a particular woman is a very valuable advantage. Exceptionally, among the Gidjingali, it is mothers and not fathers who bestow their daughters, to use Hiatt's phrase. Like other anthropologists, he observed, in this population of under 300, that when a man was looking for a wife he could not always find a girl in the relationship which would give him a claim to her; and as far as the Gidjingali were concerned, they had no conception of a continuing exchange between descent lines, though an individual man might think he had a moral right to ask for a daughter where he had given one. From the girl's point of view (or rather from that of her guardian) she might come to marriageable age at a time when there was no man with a claim to her. Men would sometimes waive their claims as an act of generosity which brought them prestige; and if an older man who already had a wife insisted on his rights against a younger unmarried man, this was not well thought of.[2]

Another example is provided by the Lele of the Kasai basin in Congo-Kinshasa.[3] They are a matrilineal people: that is to say, the children belong to their mother's clan.

2. L. Hiatt, *Kinship and Conflict*, 1965, Chapters 3 and 4.
3. M. Douglas, *The Lele of the Kasai*, 1963.

Among some such peoples the father, as the outsider marrying in, is treated with humorous banter as a mere begetter.
But among the Lele fatherhood is honoured to the point that
there is a privileged ritual association composed of fathers.
To them the begetter of daughters to perpetuate the clan has
done them the same priceless service that the kin of a woman
do in a patrilineal society when they give her in marriage. In
return he is entitled to claim the daughter of his daughter as
a wife, either for himself or for a member of his clan whom
he can choose. This is not the only case on record where the
marriage of grandfather and granddaughter is allowed in
matrilineal societies. If one assumes that it is normal for men
and women to marry at about the same age, so that most
couples are contemporaries, it seems extraordinary; but in a
society such as the Lele, where girls are married very early
and men very late, a difference of twenty years is common in
any case. Since a girl was betrothed in infancy, her husband
of the grandfather generation might die before she was
nubile, and she would then go to his heir, who would be only
'old enough to be her father'.

Arrangements of this kind have been called *delayed* exchange, as opposed to *direct* exchange when two marriages
are made at the same time. Some Arab peoples arrange marriages by direct exchange, and as these do not involve the
money payments expected in other marriages, they are particularly resorted to by poor men.[4]

In another kind of system lineages or sections of them are
linked, but not by exchange. The classic example of such a
system are the Kachins of the Burma–China frontier.[5]
Every local descent group – that is a section of a lineage
living in close enough contact to arrange marriages, like the
Tiv marriage-guardian group – is linked to at least two
others, from one of which it receives wives while it gives
wives to the other. Those who give wives are reckoned to be
the superiors of those who receive them. They call their
sons-in-law *dama*, which is the word for a vassal, and are

4. E. Marx, *Bedouin of the Negev*, 1967, p. 121.
5. E. R. Leach, *Political Systems of Highland Burma*, 1954.

called by them *mayu*, which is the word for an overlord. A headman who marries the daughter of a chief is in fact his vassal, though there is no such relationship between the commoners who form the majority of the population. The chiefs, who marry the daughters of other chiefs, are independent in their small domains and do not become one another's vassals. Instead of rendering services to their fathers-in-law or accepting their political authority they pay bridewealth, a form of exchange or equivalence about which much more will have to be said.

Leach in his account of Kachin marriage indicates that whereas ideally a *mayu–dama* relationship, once formed, should persist throughout the centuries, in practice people remember only recent alliances; or, if their memory goes further, the requirement to perpetuate the alliance is satisfied by making one marriage in each generation. It is in fact only the chiefs and headmen who seek by marriages following the ideal pattern to perpetuate their political relationship.

Marriage within the Lineage

The Arab idea that people should marry the children of a father's brother, or if not, a member of the same narrow lineage, has been mentioned as an exception to the rule of clan exogamy. It is of course also a rule of preferential marriage, and it has the effect that a man's wife may be at the same time his matrilateral cross-cousin and a member of his lineage. (But note that this is not *double* cross-cousin marriage.) This rule has never been called prescriptive, perhaps because it has been assumed that the only prescriptive marriage is that with the matrilateral cross-cousin. Like all supposedly prescriptive rules, it is invoked by the backers of a marriage that accords with it and rejected by those who oppose the marriage.

Some Arabs, such as the Bedouin of Cyrenaica described by Emrys Peters, also value, though not so highly, marriage with the matrilateral cross-cousin, and believe, like the Kachin, that where one such marriage has been made the link should be repeated in later generations. But they treat this neither as an exchange in which both sides should be equal nor as a permanent relationship of superiority and inferiority.

Among nomad Arabs the group who migrate and camp together are – or are supposed to be – members of a lineage with a common ancestor five or six generations back. Within this group degrees of kinship are visibly expressed in the order of camping, brothers close to their fathers, and even a gap in the lines where there is a gap in the genealogy. Marriages are expected to be made within this group, though the Cyrenaican cross-cousin marriage is a means of forming links outside it. In the Humr tribe of the Baggara Arabs of the Sudan, this group is called the *surra*, and consists of people who have (or think they have) a common ancestor five or six generations back. The living members, of course, really know their genealogical relationship, and divisions of them will be called 'the sons of' men still alive or remembered. It is within these small lineages that people should marry. The rule is expressed sometimes as the duty of a young man to provide for an unmarried girl, sometimes as a claim on an available wife. Duties are apt to be more elastic than claims, but it is generally recognized that a distant relative should not seek a girl in marriage unless he knows that no more closely related man wishes to do so.

From a census of marriages in one section of the Humr, I. G. Cunnison found that 17 per cent were made within the *surra* (a small one) and 36 per cent within the group of five 'brother' *surras*. In another section 36 per cent of marriages were made within the *surra* and 30 per cent with members of 'brother' *surras*. His conclusion is that 'far more marriages are contracted with the few marriageable close relatives than with the many marriageable distant relatives'.[6] But he adds that the greater proportion are first marriages, in which young people can be constrained to follow the rules. In this as in most societies where there is a preferential marriage rule, choice is freer in a second marriage, whether this

6. I. G. Cunnison, op. cit., p. 88.

follows divorce or establishes a polygamous household.

The Arab villages on the (then) Israeli border described by Abner Cohen in 1965[7] were divided into similar groups known there as *hamula*. A case which he records at length, concerning a marriage between members of two *hamulas* in the same village, shows how the rule can be differently interpreted by people with different aims. Khalid of Barham *hamula* wished to marry Fatima of Matar, with the approval of her father and brother; and it was argued that he was free to do so because all the marriageable girls in Barham were under age. But for various reasons the marriage could not be concluded at once, and in the meantime Ali, the head of Matar – as a favour to another of the senior men – asked Fatima's father for her hand on behalf of a member of the *hamula*, who, though not a close cousin, had a prior claim over an outsider. The father, despite the promises he had made to Khalid, was afraid to offend these senior men, and he took the line that the claim of the *hamula* member must prevail unless Ali could be persuaded to waive it. The head of Barham now told Khalid that there were many unmarried girls in the *hamula*, among whom he might choose; the anthropologist found that there were 17 between the ages of 17 and 35, some of whom must have been available at the time when Khalid earlier said there were none. Fatima on her side said she would not marry any man in her own *hamula*, or indeed any man but Khalid, a display of spirit that would not have been allowed in many Arab societies; as it was she was held to have brought shame on the group and was regarded as something of a portent. Then she ran away from home and took refuge with friends in another village. The issue now became one between the two *hamulas*, the Matars treating Khalid as an interloper and reacting as if he had actually abducted Fatima, an action regarded as equivalent to homicide. The quarrel became a danger to peace, and was settled in the end by the intervention of a Jewish official with twentieth-century ideas about freedom of choice in marriage.

7. A. Cohen, *Arab Border Villages in Israel*, 1965.

Much more was at stake here than the parents' choice of alliances; the marriage proposal had become entangled in a wider and more complicated quarrel between the two *hamulas*. This is something that often happens in societies where the giving of women in marriage is an important way of conducting political relationships. Indeed marriageable women can sometimes be thought of as pawns, although it does not follow that their guardians are always and entirely indifferent to their welfare. There will be more to say about this aspect of marriage in a later chapter.

Objections to Cross-Cousin Marriage

Many anthropologists who have written about 'prescribed' or 'preferred' marriages have been content to record what proportion of actual marriages follow the rules, and have often found that this is a minority; they have left it at that without asking for the reasons why the rules should be so widely disregarded. Jack and Esther Goody, however, have given the reasons for and against cross-cousin marriage that they heard from the Gonja people of northern Ghana, among whom they worked.[8] The Gonja attach much importance to maintaining relations between siblings who are divided by marriage (because the women go to their husbands' homes). One way to do this would be to arrange marriages between the children, and the Gonja are among the peoples who think this is the ideal marriage. But what they prefer to do in practice is to send small children to be brought up in a sibling's family. They are actually rather afraid of cross-cousin marriage. They believe, like many other peoples whose religion consists in a cult of their ancestors, that marital quarrels or infidelities incur the ancestors' displeasure, which they manifest by afflicting the children of the marriage with sickness. Where a couple have common ancestors the dangers from their wrath are thought to be compounded. But it is nevertheless conceived as the obligation of a mother's brother to help his sister's son to find

8. J. R. Goody, *Comparative Studies in Kinship*, 1969, pp. 229–32.

a wife; and the most straightforward way of doing this is by giving him a daughter. It is here the givers of daughters who value cross-cousin marriage, the seekers of wives who fear it.

Other reasons against cross-cousin marriage were given to Elizabeth Colson by the Plateau Tonga in Zambia. They said it was not easy to give the respect proper for a father-in-law to a man whom you had always known as an uncle – an argument that I heard myself from the Cewa in Malawi. They said too that since a dead man's heir must take responsibility for his widow by marrying her at least in form, and a man's sister's son is his heir, it was not a good thing to begin by marrying her daughter. These reasons for objection have existed as long as the rule has, and Dr Colson thinks the Tonga are beginning to raise them more often because, now that they have taken to cash farming, there is beginning to be more property to inherit. Men try to convey their property to their own children, although it should go to their sister's children, so that the children of brother and sister are apt to be competitors, more hostile than friendly.[9]

Some of the peoples that have been described in this chapter treat the giving of a woman in marriage as a service, or 'prestation', which creates an obligation to repay; the man who claims his cousin as a wife is then a sort of creditor. To others the linking of lineages by marriage is a way of maintaining political relationships. As later chapters will show, both the conception of marriage as part of an exchange of prestations and that of a son's or daughter's marriage as an alliance which should be as advantageous as possible are found in many more societies than those that value cross-cousin marriage.

9. E. M. Colson, *Marriage and the Family among the Plateau Tonga*, 1958 pp. 326–7.

CHAPTER 4

THE COST OF GETTING MARRIED

NEARLY everywhere getting married is an expensive business. But what the expense is for, who bears it, and who benefits from it may be very different in different societies. Where kinship, which springs from marriage, is the most important determinant of everyone's status and chances in life, marriage is the most important event. Many peoples regard an unmarried man as not fully adult, and this although men may have to wait for marriage for years after they have attained physical adulthood. Hence it is not surprising that marriage is usually surrounded with ceremonies at which large numbers of people are gathered, and that feasts are given for their entertainment. This is one form of expense, and there are rules about the respective obligations of the kin on the two sides in meeting it.

Another kind of expense consists in the making of presents. In the societies that are commonly called 'western' the presents come to the couple from their kin and friends and form a contribution to the equipment of the new household. In societies of simple technology they often pass between the groups which are to be linked in affinity through the marriage, the initial transfer coming from either the husband's or the wife's side. Sometimes the couple receives no share; sometimes the bride's parents give her a part of what comes to them, sometimes all of it. Transfers of goods – whether they are called gifts or payments – express the principle that Evans-Pritchard stated in the phrase 'Material objects are the chains along which social relationships run';[1] by making a gift one creates a new relationship. As Evans-Pritchard puts it elsewhere, with special reference to

[1] E. E. Evans-Pritchard, *Kinship and Marriage among the Nuer*, 1940, p. 89.

marriage, 'a gift or payment' is a 'means of establishing, defining, expressing and evoking social behaviour'.[2] There are peoples whose highest ambition is the accumulation of valued objects to be exchanged in ceremonies of gift-giving, and for them, as it would seem from the accounts of ethnographers, a marriage is important largely as an occasion for initiating such exchanges.

Then there are payments made on behalf of the husband to the man who has bestowed a wife on him, payments which are conceived as an equivalent for the services which the wife gives her husband, and are returnable if the marriage is broken. Sometimes, in lieu of such payments or in addition to them, a prospective husband works for his father-in-law, an activity which in the days of subsistence economy cost him nothing but time; nowadays when young men expect to be working for wages they give an equivalent in money. Many writers use the term *prestations* to include both payments and services. In Africa prestations are made by or on behalf of the bridegroom to the guardian of the bride (normally her father). Payments in kind may be distributed by him among his kin; often there are strict rules about who gets what. Nearly everywhere these payments are nowadays made partly or wholly in cash, and this change has had many further consequences.

Another kind of expense is the provision of dowry. But a dowry, if the word is used in its strict sense, does not pass between affines, as do the gifts and payments just described; it is property settled on the wife. Sometimes it comes entirely from the existing resources of her kin, sometimes they pass on to her a proportion – it may be a large part – of the marriage payment. The laws of some countries allow a husband to do what he likes with his wife's dowry, but essentially it is not a gift to him, still less a payment for any service. In many cases it helps to maintain the joint household, and in societies where wealth is unevenly distributed the amount of a woman's dowry makes a considerable

2. *The Position of Women in Primitive Societies and Other Essays in Social Anthropology*, 1965, p. 182.

difference to her marriage prospects. Nevertheless, it is most unfortunate that this word has been used by both French and English writers to describe the payments that are made to create a relationship of affinity.

Bridewealth

The great mass of literature referring to payments made by the husband's kin is concerned with the African custom of *bridewealth*, no doubt because Europeans first encountered it in southern Africa in the early days of the nineteenth century, and from that time on champions of African womanhood have interpreted it as a purchase that reduces the woman's status to that of a slave. Every African society where such a payment is made has a word for it. For a long time the current translation into English of all these words was 'bride-price'. In order to avoid the implications of buying and selling, Evans-Pritchard proposed as an alternative 'bridewealth', and this is now more widely used. His own work was done among the Nuer of the Southern Sudan, who make the payment in cattle, as did all the cattle-owning peoples until they began to substitute money, and the cattle payment has so many distinctive features that I prefer to limit the word 'bridewealth' to it (including the payment of cash in lieu). One reason why I think it would be desirable for this usage to be general is that when 'bridewealth' is used without further description in ethnographic accounts, the reader cannot guess whether it refers to a transfer with the distinctive consequences that the word originally implied, or simply to any form of what I shall call marriage payment. There is no need to take this word as implying the purchase of a woman. We pay attention, compliments, visits, homage, respect, in fact anything that can be thought of as due to the person to whom it is given, and not merely offered at the option of the giver. A marriage payment is the equivalent or return for something given, and in the African context it has been argued that what is given is not a woman's person but certain rights over her. These are of two kinds:

the rights that a husband has over his wife, without which there would be no marriage, and the rights that a father has over his children, which marriage does not always give him.

In any marriage a husband expects his wife to be his sexual partner and to cook and keep house for him (or organize servants for these tasks). These can be called marital rights, or the rights of a husband. They have been rather pretentiously given the half-Latin description 'rights *in uxorem*', i.e., rights *over* a wife; and this is too often translated as 'uxorial rights', which can only mean 'rights *of* a wife'.

But the question of a *father's* rights is not so simple. In a matrilineal society, although a father has the same authority as any father over children living in his house, they are not members of his lineage. They will not keep his name alive by sacrifices to his spirit, and when they are adult he has no right to control their labour or their earnings. These rights remain with their mother's lineage. They are the rights that, in a patrilineal society, are transferred at marriage.

These are the rights of *paternity*, or rights of a father (rights *in genetricem*), unfortunately too often called 'genetricial rights',[3] which can only mean the rights of a mother. It has been argued that the amount, relative to resources, that is paid by or on behalf of the bridegroom is large or small according as he is or is not gaining rights of paternity. This argument is applicable in the African context, but it is hard to apply it to cases where, although the husband is expected to make a payment, it is not this but some other part of the marriage procedure that makes the union legal and so gives him rights of paternity.

Bridewealth in Africa has traditionally been characteristic of patrilineal cattle-owning peoples. Its effect is to make the children a woman bears members of their father's lineage, and nothing else can have this effect. The tag 'Brideprice is

3. J. R. Goody, a leading authority on kinship and marriage, compounds the enormity by writing of 'their [i.e. women's] genetricial rights'. This combination of words is completely meaningless as an expression of what he is trying to say.

childprice' is a pithy expression of this fact and not, as some have supposed, a pedant's attempt at a joke. A more long-winded way of expressing the same fact is to say that it is a payment, or a gift, made in exchange for a woman's fertility. It consists in the transfer of cattle or other stock from the lineage that is to receive the woman to the lineage that gives her. Nowadays the stock, or their equivalent in money, may be produced by the bridegroom himself, but in the days when a young man had no resources outside his family or lineage patrimony he had to depend on his father's willingness to release the necessary cattle. It was a father's duty to enable his sons to marry, but at any given moment he might find a reason why the cattle were needed for some other purpose. Where the number of cattle transferred is large enough for them to be distributed among a number of households, the bulk of them will go to the woman's parents, but various other relatives will have the right to one or two beasts; if the full number are not given it is they who go without.

Both the ideal number, and the number actually given, vary widely. Ethnographers record the numbers paid in the cases they observe and thus arrive at a figure for the 'usual' payment, but they have rarely calculated the relation of this to the size of herds, still less to total resources, so that it is hard to rank different peoples in terms of 'higher or lower' bridewealth. In any case, a marriage made with bridewealth is not a market transaction, however much argument there may be – and where large numbers are given there is always plenty – about numbers and quality, how many to be paid now, how many later, and so forth. Sometimes the spokesmen of a bride's family may make much of her qualities of beauty or character, but this is in part an expression of the idea that the gift of a wife is something valuable beyond repayment, and in part just one among other moves in a contest the aim of which is to get as many cattle, or as much money, as the bridegroom's side can give without being actually impoverished. This is the reason why, as long as young men depend on the family herds for their bridewealth, only one brother can marry at a time. It is probably only among the pastoralists of remote desert regions that a man today cannot raise at least a part of his own bridewealth by working for wages, but even where it is all paid in cash it may still be raised by the father.

If the number is not fixed, or if, as sometimes happens, it is fixed at a figure that nobody can actually pay, the procedure is for the cattle that are offered to be displayed to the representatives of the bride's kin, who may reject individual animals for their poor quality, and may go on asking to see more for as long as they like. But a point will be reached when the bridegroom's representative will say, truly or not, that there are no more. It must be remembered that both parties have a pretty good idea of resources on the one side and expectations on the other.

Whether or not a standard number of cattle is regarded as the ideal, the full payment is seldom made at the time when the marriage is ceremonially concluded. The recipients are not always in a hurry to receive it, in part because this maintains the inferiority of a son-in-law and allows his father-in-law to call on him for small services, in part perhaps because of the feeling that to close an account implies cutting off a relationship, whereas the relationship of affines should be one of continuing prestations and counter-prestations. 'Bridewealth is never completed', say the Lobedu of the Transvaal. On the other hand, some fathers-in-law keep a sharp eye open for an increase in their affines' stock, and take occasion to remind them what is owing; and sickness in a family is sometimes ascribed to the anger of the mother's ancestors at remissness in paying. The main reason for a father-in-law to press for payment would be that he had difficulty in accumulating cattle for the marriage of his sons; or, among feuding peoples in the old days, that he had to pay compensation for a homicide.

Where the total number expected is small it is sometimes paid one cow at a time. This is the custom among the Tallensi of northern Ghana, where the standard number is four, and thirty years ago it was also the custom among the Nyakyusa of south-western Tanzania, although the number varied more widely there and was occasionally as many as thirty. Godfrey Wilson, who worked there in 1935, noted that most men owned a far smaller number of cattle than the total they had paid out in bridewealth at different times. At any one time a man might be in possession of ten cattle or fewer; he might have paid out at different times a total of twenty times as much. Here an unmarried man receives cattle one by one from his father when he is held to have done enough work in his father's fields (though not of course at a wage). If he has chosen the girl he wants to marry he passes them on to her father; if not, or perhaps even if he has, he may get involved in compensation payments for adultery, and this will postpone his marriage.

It should have become clear by now that cattle are not a general medium of exchange but a means of establishing and maintaining particular social relationships. They are given in marriage in return for a woman, and they are paid in compensation to injured humans and in sacrifice to angry spirits. The compensation for homicide among the Nuer is ideally equivalent to the bridewealth, and is supposed to enable the descent group that has lost a man to make a new marriage and thus fill his place. Nor are cattle a *mere* medium of exchange; they are prized for their own sake and for the milk they give, and every owner of a herd rejoices to see its numbers increase. Yet they circulate so constantly that bridewealth cannot be thought of as a source of accumulation. The reason is obvious: daughters are *sought* in marriage, but sons must *find* wives. Whenever a herd-owning group has enough cattle to do so, it should make a marriage; and since polygynous marriage is permitted and valued, there is always someone who wishes to marry.

It is the duty of a father to enable his sons to marry before he marries additional wives himself. This is also the duty of his heir if he should die leaving unmarried sons, but elder brothers, and particularly elder half-brothers, are sometimes less conscientious than fathers, and this is often a cause of fraternal dissension.

One way of making provision is to pair brothers with sisters, so that the bridewealth received for one girl is allocated to the marriage of a particular boy. This may be held to put him under a continuing obligation to his sister, as it does with the Lobedu. This woman is said to have 'established his house', and in return she can claim a daughter of this house as the wife for her son. The effect is simply to establish a relationship between descent groups similar to that of the Kachins, one always receiving brides from one side and giving brides to the other. But it is rationalized in a remarkable way, in that a daughter of the cattle-linked brother is thought of as making a return to the *woman* whose cattle created the 'house', and making this return by cooking and 'grinding mealies' for her as a daughter-in-law would. And this woman can claim the girl even if there is no son to marry her. Of course the 'son' need not be a first cousin, though he often is; in 60 per cent of the cases, according to the Kriges, who have given us our account of the Lobedu.[4] These cousins are said to be 'born for' one another, and a girl cannot choose another husband in preference; nor could such a man offer himself as a suitor. Whereas Nyende women constrained by exchange rules leave their husbands for other men,[5] Lobedu women, who cannot legally marry elsewhere, engage in illicit amours, which the Kriges regard as a concession to realities and the Lobedu accept provided they are discreet.

Another way of apportioning bridewealth cattle is that of the Nyakyusa. In a polygynous family such as every man hopes to found, brothers claim a prior right to the cattle received for their full sisters. But they cannot count on having an equal number of sisters, and their father can readjust the balance by transferring a cow to the 'house' of another wife. This is regarded as a debt to be repaid in due course; but it also lays the foundation for a continuing series of exchanges which, like the exchanges between affines, are thought to confirm and strengthen the links between the

4. E. J. and J. D. Krige, *The Realm of a Rain Queen*, 1943, p. 144.
5. See Chapter 3.

houses. The transfer is made for its own sake; a father seeks to create such a link between his eldest son and the eldest son of any other wife whom he may later marry.

For a long time now, in those parts of Africa where money circulates freely, bridewealth has been offered or demanded in money instead of cattle. When this is done the cash equivalent of a beast may be treated as a fixed amount, as it is by the Lobedu in the Transvaal, who for at least fifty years have reckoned the value at £5. If then people continue to describe the payment in terms of numbers of cattle, they will simply ask 'more cattle' from a man whose income they suppose will stand it. Anthropologists who have worked where bridewealth is paid wholly in cash tell us very little about the process of reaching agreement, though they remark on some of the consequences of the change. Handing over a sum of money clearly cannot be done with the dramatic publicity that accompanies the driving of cattle from one village or homestead to another. The passage of shillings or pound notes from one hand to the next is not and cannot be followed with the same close interest as the movement of cattle, every one of which is recognized individually, as successive marriages are made. Moreover, it is impossible to insist that cash received as bridewealth should be paid out only in bridewealth. It is true that bridewealth cattle might often have been sold to raise cash, but in fact they were not; again, the process would have been too conspicuous. It is also true that men who received cattle in bridewealth did not always meet their obligations to their agnates; a father might marry a second wife while he had a son still wifeless, and an elder brother would be very likely to treat his younger brothers this way. But when bridewealth can be disposed of in an infinite number of alternative ways the possibility of a conflict of interests is so much the greater.

As to the actual bargaining over the amount to be paid, very few ethnographers tell us much. The Gisu in north-eastern Uganda still discuss whether they will offer or accept cattle or money, and there, where only three or four cattle were ever paid, argument turns on their current market price. An astute bargainer can defeat attempts to raise the figure by offering the cow itself instead of money. If the various gifts customarily made to individuals, for example to the bride's mother as an expression of gratitude for bringing her up, are replaced by cash, arguments begin about just what is to be taken as included in the sum offered — and from there the discussion goes on to how much of this is to be returned if there is a divorce. Of course, a bride's guardian does not put the money in the bank to be available if the marriage breaks up, just as he did not carefully keep the cattle for the same reason; but whereas he would almost certainly use the cattle to get a wife for one of her brothers, he is just as likely to use the money, a larger lump sum than he ever receives in any other way, for some major outlay such as a corrugated iron roof for his own house.

The kind of haggling that takes place when the payment is made in cash may be illustrated from the Nyoro, of whom it is reported that the cash value of the goods still given in kind (beer and a goat) is played down so that more cash can be demanded to make up the total payment. Then comes the haggling over the amount of this. In one case the bridegroom's representative offered 200 shillings, the bride's father demanded 400. Eventually he said, 'If in accordance with the custom of our country you will help me by seeing that I receive presents of salt, sugar and so on from time to time, you may bring 270 shillings over and above the goat and the beer.' Later he knocked a little more off the total.[6]

There is no denying that the marriage of a daughter can now be made a means of raising ready money as often as it is a means of gaining useful affines. This no more makes her a 'slave' than the traditional system did; fathers may sell, but husbands do not buy. Nevertheless, sad and sordid tales are told of incidents that could not have happened in the days of the cattle payment. Thus a Bete man in the Ivory Coast needed to raise a large sum of money and did so by accepting a marriage payment for his daughter. He then refused to let

6. J. H. M. Beattie, unpublished field material.

her go to the man who had made the payment; the latter seized her and told her father he could repay the money if he wanted her back. We are not told whether the girl herself was unwilling. A Nyoro case is sadder: a young girl was married to an older man whom she could not endure, but her father had 'eaten' the bridewealth and could not release her. The girl hanged herself. But it is possible for some women nowadays to earn money and release themselves.

If the essence of the bridewealth system lies in the circulation of cattle, those received for one marriage being used to make another, one may wonder how it has been possible now for so many generations for the system of cash payment to be kept up. The answer seems to be that men now earn cash for themselves and do not depend on their sisters' marriages.

Bridewealth as Child-Price

'Bride-price is child-price'. Some of the effects of the payment that are summed up in this sentence are apt to be surprising to beginners in anthropology. They can be subsumed under the rule that nothing can dissolve a marriage created by a cattle payment except the return of the cattle; not even the death of the husband. If we recall that the bridewealth is essentially a return made for the woman's fertility we can see that its significance is in determining the lineage status of the children she bears. 'The children are where the cattle are not' is a South African saying. What this means is that as long as the cattle given on a man's behalf are in the possession of a woman's lineage (or rather, have not been returned, since it has been shown that they quickly pass further) the children she bears are counted as the children of that man. She may run away with a lover; this makes no difference. When her husband dies she should go to his heir (this is called *leviratic* marriage). Often this is not insisted upon, but if she chooses to live with another man the children she bears to him are still those of her dead husband.

An even more remarkable custom is recognized by the

Nuer and by some peoples in South Africa: what Evans-Pritchard has called 'ghost marriage'. If a man dies unmarried, or after a marriage which has given him no male child or sons who died as children, some close kinsman ought to marry a wife 'to his name'; the children of this marriage will be accounted the descendants of the dead man and so keep his name alive and have it reckoned among the ancestors. The man who performs this duty may not be able to marry a second wife who would be *his* wife and bear *his* children; so when *he* dies a kinsman ought in his turn to make a ghost marriage on *his* behalf. Evans-Pritchard reckoned that there must be among the Nuer almost as many ghost marriages as ordinary marriages. In such a marriage the husband's position in everyday life is exactly the same as any other husband's. He is the family authority and he has all a father's responsibilities towards the children his wife bears, including providing cattle for the sons to marry. Only they are not his children.

This is a convenient place to note the distinction that anthropologists make between the pater and the genitor. (Latin words again, but we use these correctly and no longer treat them like foreigners.) The genitor is the *actual* begetter, the pater the man to whose line the children belong, or, as Malinowski called him, the *social* father. In these terms bridewealth makes a man the pater of all children borne by the woman for whom it has been given. And it can also make a woman so, paradoxically as this may seem. 'Woman-marriage', as Evans-Pritchard has called it, is by no means an uncommon custom. A woman can pay bridewealth for another woman, and this has the same jural consequences as a marriage of man and woman: the wife and children are under the authority of the 'female husband', she has the right to damages if the wife commits adultery, and the children belong to the 'husband's' lineage, that is the natal lineage of the woman. The woman, in anthropological terms, is the pater. She must of course provide a genitor to perform the sexual part of her role; this would probably be some poor kinsman.

According to Evans-Pritchard's account of the Nuer, it is usually barren women who make such marriages, and indeed it is hard to imagine a woman who had her own children doing so. Such women are in some ways assimilated to men, and may receive the share due to a male relative in the bride-wealth of a daughter of their lineage. Also they frequently practise as diviners or purveyors of medicines, and are rewarded for their services with cattle; this is how they can build up herds of their own.

The Lobedu are among the people who recognize this kind of marriage. This is to be expected, since they see cross-cousin marriage as a way of returning a servant (in the shape of a daughter-in-law) to the woman who by the cattle that her marriage brought in made possible the marriage of her brother. Suppose such a woman has no son to whom her brother might give a daughter; she is allowed to 'marry' the girl herself. She will not own any cattle (or cash), so her husband provides the bridewealth for this 'marriage'. Moreover, the son who never existed might have been the heir to some position of political importance. In that case the girl who has been 'married' by her aunt must bear a son to take his place; a man is allotted to beget this son, though he does not attain the status of husband to the girl. This is a kind of ghost marriage as well as 'woman-marriage'.

These rules achieve two ends which are similar but not identical: the desire to have *descendants* and the desire to have *children*. The first can be explained, as it is in many societies, by the wish to be the object of an ancestor cult, to be tended in the other world by the offerings of one's descendants; only direct descendants make offerings to individual ancestors. But it is also felt in societies where ancestor cults are not very important, and perhaps it simply expresses that wish for continuity that seems to be deeply rooted in human nature. The second is more practical in societies where the household is a working team. Children are loved in most societies, but in pre-industrial societies they are not merely objects of aesthetic and emotional satisfaction: they are the means to wealth for the fortunate and an insurance against old age for everyone. A father has the right to the labour of his sons, and often also control over wealth that they acquire by their individual efforts. Girls stay with their mothers and work with them, but the father has the right to their bridewealth. From the point of view of the sons their patrimony is that of the man who has paid bridewealth for their mother. If it is thought shocking in these days of individual freedom that men should have such rights over their children, we might reflect that arguments over foster-children in this country still turn on the question of the 'rights' of 'natural parents' (which in this context means legally married parents).

The significance of 'bride-price' as 'child-price' is made very clear in the Nuer rules for the return of the cattle in case of divorce or the death of a wife. If she dies leaving one child a part only of the bridewealth is returned; if she leaves her husband he may claim the return of all his cattle except six, which are held to establish his rights in the child. It was said also that if a wife who had borne two children left her husband her kinsmen would refuse to return any cattle. But this would be equivalent to refusing to let him divorce her; her later children would be reckoned as his.

In matrilineal societies it is not marriage that enables a man to continue his line of descent. It is his sisters who do this. His wife is a sexual and domestic companion. What he gets from marriage is the status of a household head, though sometimes only a subordinate household head in her father's homestead (or her mother's brother's). It is to be expected, then, that payment to her kin should not bulk as large in the contraction of a marriage as it does where 'bride-price' is 'child-price'. But whereas one can say that all patrilineal peoples have (more or less) the same marriage arrangements, every matrilineal society seems to be unique. If we look at the peoples of the 'matrilineal belt' which runs across central Africa we find that the Bemba, among whom traditionally both boys and girls were betrothed as children, expected a small payment (two barkcloths and a hoe) when the marriage was first agreed upon, some years of service from the boy, and another payment at the girl's puberty ceremony, which immediately preceded her marriage. The final payment established the husband's status as a recognized father, the consequence of which was to give him the right to be consulted in the marriages of his children. The Tonga to the south-west of them traditionally made two payments, one of a hoe and a spear, the other of five more hoes, which were returned if there was a divorce. It was this that entitled the man to recognition as the head of an independent household; and until it had been paid, he could not expect any co-operation from his wife's kin if she ran away or he considered that she was otherwise misbehaving. When the Tonga began to keep cattle, something that is rare among matrilineal peoples, cattle were substituted for the hoes, and when Elizabeth Colson was there in 1950 the payment, the amount of which was agreed upon at the time of betrothal, was often not completed until two children had been born.

Another matrilineal people, also called Tonga, in the north of Malawi, make payments entirely in cash, one to seal betrothal and another to make the marriage valid (but some do not make them at all, a point to be discussed later in relation to the procedure for getting married). A man who has made the payment agreed on with his wife's guardian is entitled to claim the payments made for his daughters.

In West Africa the Akan-speaking peoples of Ghana are the best known example of matriliny. There too relatively small cash gifts are made to the bride herself and individuals among her close kin. But what makes the marriage legal is a present of drink (or money to pay for it) made to either the girl's father or her lineage guardian, who share it whichever first receives it. This 'thanks money' is what is given at the sealing of any contract. It is consumed on the spot, unlike cattle which remain for some time as evidence that the marriage is in being, and are remembered much longer. If there is a divorce it is ratified by a return gift of the same kind from the wife's side, but there is no question of balancing this against the number of children.

In the African context anthropologists have sought to correlate the high or low cost of marriage payments with the nature of the rights acquired by husbands – high when they gain the children as lineage members, low when they do not. This is a more precise way of putting the difference than by speaking of acquiring or not acquiring rights of paternity, for paternity is always recognized in some way.

Other Types of Payment

But there are other societies, in other respects widely different, in which a payment or prestation, whichever word is thought more apt, is an indispensable part of marriage procedure yet is not the essential legalizing act and does not affect the status of the children. In these societies the predominant idea of a marriage seems to be that it initiates or confirms an alliance that will be maintained by an endless series of exchanges, an idea that is present in African marriages, but there is not emphasized nearly so much; or one might put it that there, although the giving of the woman creates or confirms the alliance, rights over her are not reckoned among the prestations exchanged.

The marriage payments made in the highlands of New Guinea consist of pearl shells, pigs and plumes of rare birds. Sometimes these are treated by anthropologists as if they closely resembled bridewealth, and sometimes as if they were very different. Thus Salisbury, writing of the Siane near Goroka, says that a part of the valuables received at a girl's marriage are put into her brother's marriage payment, but this, according to his observations, was normally only one third of the total.[7] He says that if a woman leaves her husband after bearing two children she is held to have 'repaid' the marriage payment, and no demand would be made on her kin, a rule which might be paralleled in many parts of Africa. But where New Guinea differs from Africa is that, even if the payment can be balanced in that way against the children whom the woman bears, it is also expected to be balanced by a repayment of equivalent goods at

7. R. F. Salisbury, *From Stone to Steel*, 1962, p. 98.

the time when the bride goes to her husband, and in order to make this possible the two sides agree in advance on a suitable amount. Also, whenever a child is born a further gift must be made to the woman's kin, without which, it seems, they would still be held to have claims over the children; whereas in Africa bridewealth settles their paternity once and for all. Moreover, although a woman living with a man who has made no payment is not considered to be married at all, the kin of a married woman may accept a payment from a new husband without annulling the first marriage by returning the original payment. Indeed it seems that such a return is held to be a matter of recompense to the husband for his loss rather than a formal way of ending a marriage.

The peculiarity of New Guinea marriage payments is that they have an aspect which is really independent of the marriage itself; the first marriage presentation links the new affines as partners in the elaborate ceremonial exchanges through which men acquire prestige, and they should then continue to exchange gifts on occasions unconnected with the marriage. In most African bridewealth marriages, divorce can only be accomplished by the return of the bridewealth. The woman's kin, who hold it, are expected to try to patch up the quarrel, and the rights and wrongs on either side are the sole consideration. But in New Guinea, as Meggitt puts it, a woman who wants a divorce 'must convince her agnates that the gravity of her husband's offence outweighs the socio-economic advantage of his exchange relations with them'.[8] If a return is made, the amount of the original gift is included in calculating how much is due. The function of the original payment as legalizing the marriage cannot be disentangled from its function in the chain of ceremonial exchange.

It is obvious that where the bride and bridegroom are expected to be members of the same lineage there is no room for prestations of bridewealth type, which make a woman's children members of her husband's line. So the marriage payments of nomad Arabs are of a different nature. Islam

8. M. J. Meggitt, *The Lineage System of the Mae-Enga*, 1965, p. 143.

prescribes that to make a marriage legal a man must make his bride a gift known as *mahar*, a word that scholars translate as 'dower' (not dowry), because it is an endowment of the bride and becomes her personal property. But in many parts of Africa a payment is still made to the woman's parents although this has none of the functions of bridewealth. Thus the Baggara of Sudan make a cash payment to the bride's mother, most of which she keeps to spend on cloth or small luxuries, though she may buy sheep which are then kept for her daughter's children. The bridegroom, or his kin, also directly provide household gear, clothing and silver ornaments for the bride.[9] Somali make a betrothal gift to the girl's parents, but the later prestations do not go all in one direction. They are exchanged between the two families, or, more precisely, about two-thirds of the camels given from the husband's side are returned. With these camels sometimes go horses and rifles, which are greatly prized and are not returned. With the camels from the wife's side come mats and skins to build the portable hut, and pots and pans to furnish it.[10]

In an Arab village in Tunisia, which has been somewhat impressionistically described by a French sociologist,[11] large cash payments are made by a man to his wife's family, who are normally in another village. One man had married several times and each time had sold date palms until he had none left. The woman's parents endow her with jewels, which are passed from mother to daughter. Although in this old-fashioned village no woman would dream of selling her jewels, in the towns they are a source of cash and make women to some extent independent of their husbands.

At a Chinese wedding too, before the days of Mao Tsetung, a bridegroom's family sealed his betrothal, which might have been arranged while he was a young boy, with substantial gifts of clothing, jewellery, food and sometimes

9. I. G. Cunnison, op. cit., p. 95.

10. I. M. Lewis, *Marriage and the Family in Northern Somaliland*, 1962, pp. 14–16.

11. J. Duvignaud, *Change at Shebika*, 1970.

T–C

cash. These were interpreted as an expression of thanks to the girl's family for having brought her up, and they were entitled to protest if they thought the amount inadequate. But when she eventually went to her husband she often took back the clothing and jewellery.[12] In a Turkish village described by Paul Stirling, the trousseau consists of mattresses and bedding, donkey bags and rugs, as well as clothing, and presents of clothes are made as well to the bridegroom and his kin. The trousseau is publicly displayed at the homes of both the bride and the groom, and naturally the family prestige depends on its amount. Villagers said a girl's father was always out of pocket although he received a cash gift from the husband. Stirling interprets the latter gift as an expression of thanks to the women of the bride's family for their labour in making the trousseau,[13] but says that it too is essentially a form of conspicuous consumption, of demonstrating what the husband's father can afford.

The expenses of a marriage in northern India are of quite a different type. Here what is most important for the status of children is the caste membership of their parents, and it is hardly possible to make a marriage which will be formally approved and blessed with the appropriate ritual unless the couple are of the same caste. No question arises of payment for the right to count children as the members of one's descent group, nor is there anything that can be described as payment for the wife's sexual and domestic services. An orthodox Hindu father *offers* his daughter as a bride, gives a dowry with her, and after the marriage is expected to go on sending presents to her husband's family. This has been regarded as analogous to the tribute from an inferior to a superior who gives protection in return. It would be hard to interpret every marriage in an Indian village literally in that way, but it is the fact that where a caste is subdivided the ideal is that a girl should marry a man from the division next higher in rank than her own. This is known as *hypergamy*, and it will be further discussed in the following chapter. This rule has the effect of limiting the number of men who are

12. M. Freedman, *Rites and Duties*, 1967, p. 13.
13. P. Stirling, *Turkish Village*, 1965, p. 188.

highly eligible as husbands. It does not make it difficult for girls to marry at all, since the less fortunate can marry their equals, but it means that a higher caste bridegroom can be said to 'have his price'.

However, what is more interesting in Oscar Lewis's and other accounts is that the amount a girl's parents are expected to spend on the wedding feast is far more than what they give the girl herself as dowry. It is on the one hand a matter of prestige to be able to give a large feast, and on the other a way of honouring the family of the bridegroom. Both the scale of the feast – the number of people to be invited – and the amount of the dowry have to be agreed between the two families, but according to Lewis the former question is the more difficult. He mentions a man who was determined that there should be a hundred guests at his son's wedding, and rejected a number of proposals before he was able to achieve this. The largest dowry that he recorded was 650 rupees, whereas weddings cost between 1,100 and 2,000.[14]

Return gifts are made from the groom's side, and Adrian Mayer, writing of central India,[15] says that the expenses on both sides are about equal, though of course this does not mean that each side gets back what it gives. The major expense on the boy's side is the hire of bullock carts for the procession that goes to fetch the bride. He reckons the cost of a wedding at six to twelve months' income. He uses the term dowry for a payment made to the groom's father, and Lewis seems to include in it also gifts distributed among his kin. This would give the word a very different meaning from what it has in Europe.

T. N. Madan, who has made one of the best analyses of Indian marriage prestations in his study of a Kashmiri village, does not interpret the dowry payment as an anticipated inheritance, and this interpretation could not be accepted in a system where women have no formal inheritance rights. But he does say that they indirectly compensate a girl for her 'loss' of such rights (which, supposedly, she would have retained had she remained within her own family? Here we

14. O. Lewis, *Village Life in Northern India*, 1958.
15. A. C. Mayer, *Caste and Kinship in Central India*, 1960.

come up against the rather difficult notion of compensation for an event that, far from being abnormal, is expected and desired). He adds that the amount given in all prestations taken together is a matter of prestige for both the families linked by the marriage, and that if it is large it enhances the girl's standing and popularity in her new home.[16] Of course we must remember that in an Indian joint family, where the senior man controls all its resources, the dowry need not in fact be devoted to the benefit of the girl who brings it or even of her own children.

A bride-price (*not* bridewealth) is sometimes paid among the less orthodox Pahari in the foothills of the Himalayas. It is a cash payment, and goes to the wedding expenses of the bride's family. In a marriage concluded in this way the bride takes with her no dowry, or only a token gift. It is recognized that it is contrary to high-caste rules for anything to be given in exchange for the bride, and it seems that the 'bride-price' is only accepted by families which could not meet the wedding expenses without it, nor give their child a dowry. But it is discussed, both by advocates and opponents, in terms of a payment for the girl. 'How can you sell a daughter you love?' ask its critics. 'We don't accept charity. When we take a girl we pay for her,' say its defenders.[17]

Some readers may be asking how, in such a system, poor people ever get married at all. The answer is that if you are willing to let your poverty be publicly seen there are ways of avoiding the elaborations that high-caste and/or rich men set store by. But because most people try to keep up with the Joneses – and they must if they want their daughters to make a good match – many get into debt.

Dowry

Etymologically the words *dowry* and *dower* are associated with an endowment of somebody with property. *Dower*, the less common word, is used for the gifts of property made to a

16. T. N. Madan, *Family and Kinship*, 1965.
17. G. D. Berreman, *Hindus of the Himalayas*, 1963, pp. 128–9.

bride from her husband or his kin in Islamic societies. *Dowry*
describes more appropriately property which her own family
bestow on her. One sometimes meets with the idea that
dowry is a sort of reversed bride-price; where wives are
scarce, husbands pay, where husbands are scarce, fathers-in-
law pay. One even occasionally comes across the word
'groom-price'. This is the reason for discussing dowry in this
context; it *is* one of the expenses of marriage, though not in
this case the husband's, and it *is* a matter of discussion, and
argument, when a marriage is being arranged. And where a
dowry is expected, no husband is likely to forgo it. But
dowry is nowhere necessary to make a marriage legal or to
establish paternity.

In so-called *cognatic* societies, where people inherit property from both parents, it is very common for both partners
at the time when they marry to receive their share of their
parents' land and household goods, and the woman's share
could appropriately be called a dowry.

In sixteenth-century England, however, this transfer of
property to a woman at marriage was called, more literally,
her 'portion'. The marriages of aristocrats in England at that
period were much concerned with amassing and retaining
landed property, and the arrangements expected to be made
at such a marriage represent the other end of a scale that
begins with the allotment of one or two fields when peasant
rice-farmers marry. A sixteenth-century nobleman gave his
daughter a 'portion' in cash, as well as her outfit of clothing
and jewels. But her husband's father had also to make provision for her in the form of a 'jointure' which would support
her if she was left a widow. This was usually done by ear-
marking for her a portion of the land that her husband
would inherit. Marriage negotiations turned largely on the
relative value of the contributions from the two sides. The
groom's father also undertook to maintain his son; not, as
would happen automatically in Africa, by allowing the new
wife to cultivate some of his patrimony in land, but either by
guaranteeing him a cash income or by giving him a house
and land from which he would derive an income. This might

be the property earmarked for the wife's jointure. When the couple were first married – and both might be very young – they might live with the husband's parents while the wife learned housekeeping and they accumulated furniture for their own house. The historian from whom this interesting information comes, unfamiliar with societies outside Europe, is distressed to think of them beginning their married life under the eyes of interfering parents.[18]

But where dowry is more than the anticipation of an inheritance that would come to a woman in any case, it is the price, not of any husband but of a particular husband. In this sense it may be compared, despite the differences, with an unusually high bridewealth which might be paid to secure, not a particular girl but a particular father-in-law. Nur Yalman shows how, among the Sinhalese, dowry is linked with *hypergamy* – the marriage of a woman to a man of higher status that is widely approved in India and Ceylon. When equals marry no dowry is given, but if the girl's family are gaining the advantage of an influential or high-class alliance, they are expected to give something for it. The dowry may be all in cash or may include houses and land, and it is transferred to the daughter by her parents in a signed document. Her husband has the management of it, of course, but if he can afford to do without the produce he may let his wife's brothers go on using it. The Sinhalese see this not as a bargain but a matter of self-respect; the girl must not be beholden to her husband or he would treat her as a servant. But of course they also see the advantages of having useful in-laws, and many think that to acquire such an advantage it is worth while to give a dowry which impoverishes them.[19]

Dowry payments have most often been considered, however, in a European context; indeed, it is because Europeans are familiar with the word that they have misapplied it in reference to Africa. A number of anthropologists have dis-

18. L. Stone, 'Marriage among English Nobility', *Journal of Comparative Studies in Society and History*, 1960. I am indebted for this reference to Dr Peter Loizos.

19. N. Yalman, *Under the Bo Tree*, 1967, pp. 172ff.

cussed its significance among Greek peasants (including Cypriots), and have shown how, given the recognition of a general principle that a woman should be endowed by her parents when she marries, there is a balance between the material value of the endowment and the social or prestige value of the husband. This has the effect, which is produced in other societies by other means, that most marriages take place between families of roughly equivalent wealth and status. But every arranged marriage is arranged with an eye to the advantages to be expected from the new relationship, and dowry can sometimes attract a husband of somewhat higher status than the bride. Men can set a price on themselves in a much more explicit way than is ever done in the discussion of bridewealth for a woman. In the Greek village of Vasilika, as it is described by Ernestine Friedl, the crucial question in arranging a marriage is often what minimum the man will accept, and this although, as in other European societies, it is the man who is supposedly seeking the hand of the woman. The husband will of course also be made aware of whatever advantages there may be in association with his wife's family.

(In Vasilika, the villagers actually talk of 'viewing the bride' as some Africans hold a 'cattle-view'. Of course it is only a coincidence that different writers have used the same word in translating from different languages, but it is an amusing coincidence.)

Although the word hypergamy was coined to refer to caste societies, it is beginning to be used in the more general context or dowry payment, and it is certainly appropriate in Vasilika. There all parents hope to marry their daughters to men in town, who have occupations of higher prestige, can give their wives a comfortable life and use their influence on behalf of their in-laws in such matters as finding them jobs.

Although it is wrong to think of dowry payments as arising in situations where it is difficult for a woman to find a husband at all, such a situation may exist as, for example, in a Cyprus village described by Peter Loizos. The Cypriots expect to find their marriage partners within the village, but there is still room for judging the relative merits or prospects of various possible sons-in-law. Also there has in recent years been a change in the sex ratio so that women are now in the majority. Loizos ascribes to this the great increase in the amount that men expect in dowry; in particular the fact that it is now expected to provide the cost of a house for the couple, which previously came from the husband. A house costs £2,000, whereas a Cypriot peasant can expect at best an income of £500.

In Greece, as in India, a father's obligation is to get husbands for his daughters, and this is the major preoccupation of the whole family. Men should not seek wives until their sisters are provided for, and they must be expected to collect the amount that will be needed by saving over years. It is true that when a man comes to marry he will be able to make terms about the dowry he will take, but since a dowry stays with the bride (and her husband, naturally), it does not directly provide the means for the receiving family to make a new marriage as bridewealth does. As is natural, men remember more vividly their own efforts to provide for their sisters than those other people have made to provide for their wives; and if you have many more sisters than brothers you are indeed unfortunate. Friedl says that in Vasilika parents limit their families with the need to endow their daughters in mind, but this is by no means usual in dowry-paying societies.

These various types of outlay on marriage are related to the different aspects of that central institution which are emphasized in different societies, but it is not possible, at any rate in the present state of knowledge, to make simple correlations. African payers of bridewealth are concerned with the perpetuation of the lineage. The Chinese are, or have been until recently, equally concerned with the lineage, but they do not pay bridewealth. For Africans and for Kachins, a wife is a gift for which hardly any return is adequate. In the New Guinea Highlands she seems to be the mere token of a partnership for the exchange of gifts. Mediterranean payers of dowry may once have been interested simply in doing their share towards the establishment of a new household, but for them dowry has become a means of raising the status of their children; whenever dowry is paid, daughters, though they may be the link with influential sons-in-law, are a liability, to be 'married off'. The latent hostility that is everywhere felt towards affines is dramatically expressed in the ostentation of an Indian wedding, where the hospitality offered supposedly marks the opening of a friendly relationship. The one common factor in all these various examples is the principle that gifts and hospitality create as well as symbolize social relationships.

CHAPTER 5

MARRIAGE STRATEGY

A HARD-HEADED attitude towards marriage is to be expected in societies where anyone's chances in life depend more on his kinship ties than on other circumstances, and where the wealth and status that he acquires by birth are more important than any of his own achievements – *except* an alliance with useful affines. This is a characteristic of most non-industrial societies and even of the agricultural sector of many of them.

Women are disposed of by their male guardians. Men are more often free to make their own choice, though the consent of their seniors is necessary, for practical if for no other reasons, when a large bridewealth or other payment has to be raised. But marriages may be arranged in childhood for boys as well as for girls, and one can then say that they too are pawns in the marriage game. Such arrangements are purely a matter of making appropriate alliances, either those indicated by the rules of preferred marriage or those in which there is an advantage to be gained from some affinal connection. In the betrothal of children there can be little question of personal characteristics, either of the type that elders approve or that young people find attractive.

One can always speak then of the disposal of women, and, in the case of preferred marriages, of claims to women, a description that seems in most cases more realistic than the older notion that it is a man's duty to marry the appropriate relative. That may occasionally be so, but case-histories do not often show us people treating marriage plans from the point of view of a man's obligation.

Women as Pawns

There are peoples among whom women may be literally pawns. An example are the Lele of the Kasai basin in Congo-Kinshasa who have been described by Dr Mary Douglas. She believes that their custom of pawning was once much more widespread in Central Africa.

It was a rule among the Lele that anyone who caused another's death owed a debt to his clan; this was more often a matter of causing death by mystical means than of physical homicide. If a woman died in giving birth it was supposed that she must have been guilty of adultery, and her lover was liable for blood-payments. So was anyone convicted by ordeal of causing a death by sorcery. Blood-debts were paid in women. A woman so transferred became the *pawn* of the injured group, and her descendants shared this status, so that the daughters were disposed of in marriage by the clan of her 'lords' and not by their own clansmen.

In a remote part of Cameroun, near the western border, live a people called Bangwa who also recognize the right of certain persons other than kinsmen to dispose of women in marriage.[1] The relationship of a girl to such a man may be called wardship, using the word that describes such a relationship in English law; the man concerned is called her *tangkap*, a word derived from *ngkap*, which means 'wealth' and specifically 'bridewealth'. In the past the Bangwa were active traders in slaves, and a girl's *tangkap* is supposedly the descendant of the man who bought the female slave from whom she is herself descended. Thus it could be argued logically that all Bangwa women have a slave status, and some might seek to extend the argument further and see in this situation evidence for the assertion that African marriage is a form of slavery. Yet the *tangkap* does not in any sense *own* his ward himself; what he has is the right to take her for his son or give her to a henchman whom he wishes to favour. Her parents must give their consent, but if the *tangkap* is

1. R. Brain, 'Bangwa (Western Bamileke) Marriage Wards', *Africa*, 1969, pp. 11–22.

their political superior, as often happens, they are not likely to refuse it.

'Wardships,' a chief said to Robert Brain, 'are our money.' His share of marriage payments form a large part of a chief's income (as well as payments on the death of both male and female wards), and the servants of an important chief with many wards spend much of their time travelling around the country making sure that nobody is concealing a marriage from which he should profit. A commoner can offer a wardship (*not a woman*) to a chief in payment of some claim. A *tangkap* is *expected* to take a benevolent interest in his wards, and if the ward is the child of a recently purchased slave (which is still possible) and so has no extended family, he may actually become the guardian; as in any society, a trustee may or may not adequately carry out his trust. Nowadays he is expected to help with his ward's education.

The emancipators who believe that the status of an African wife is identical with that of a slave have concentrated their fire on Cameroun in recent years, and since the *tangkap* institution is actually derived from a relationship between owners and slaves, they might well find ammunition there for their arguments. But they would be forgetting that, even if one were to say the ward is the slave of her *tangkap* (which would hardly describe her actual situation), his right to arrange her marriage does *not* make her the slave of her *husband*.

This case is quoted because it would immediately bring to a historian's mind the wardship system in sixteenth-century England, when the Tudors took advantage of a feudal law to increase their revenues. In feudal times a vassal held land from the king in return for military service. If he died and left an heir who was too young to render this service, the king temporarily took back the land and took charge of the heir during his minority; this is what wardship meant in England. The king was responsible for the upbringing of the ward; he might be more concerned with political loyalty than with schooling, but that is another story. In England a women could inherit, and the king was entitled to control the marriages of female wards, and allotted them to favoured vassals as any African chief would.

Tudor kings were not concerned to exercise such close control, but they were hard put to it for revenues in an age when taxation was not taken for granted. Henry VII revived a number of feudal claims which now had a cash value. The value of wardships lay in the right of the guardian to receive one third of the land inherited by the ward and to control the ward's marriage. People would pay large sums for these rights, and the income of the Court of Wards came during the reign of Elizabeth to form a substantial part of the Crown's revenue. The aim of the guardian was to marry the ward to a member of his family and to unite their lands; with just the same intention he would seek to arrange the marriages of his own children. The sale of wardships was one of the abuses that the Parliamentarians attacked, but the Court of Wards was not abolished until 1660.

An arranged marriage is usually made with other advantages in mind than the character of the partners as this is evaluated by their future affines, though parents or guardians commonly claim to be the best judges of this too. The question of marriage strategy concerns the type of consideration that the makers of such marriages have in mind. In all this discussion we are concerned with first marriages; when a man takes an additional wife in a polygynous society, and when either a man or woman remarries after divorce, there is usually much greater freedom of choice. Many marriages are arranged by the betrothal of children, even sometimes the promise of unborn children. If such a couple separate, as happens fairly often, the circumstances in which they find new mates will clearly be different.

Marriage strategy can operate in one of two situations: where it is hard for a man to find a wife, and where it is hard for a woman to find a husband. The first is more characteristic of societies which permit polygyny; it is there that the right to 'bestow' women is most valued, though it is not only there that men in appropriate kinship categories can assert claims on particular women as wives. It is rare to find unmarried women in a polygynous society, although some have rules of conduct which disqualify a woman from marriage if she breaks them. In monogamous societies there may be a surplus of women, but even there most women's guardians are concerned not merely to get them married at any price but to marry them well – that is to husbands who will be useful affines. It is not only European societies that are monogamous, but the question of what standard of living a husband can give his wife – which of course is also considered by her parents – is more significant in societies where there are appreciable differences in income.

The Politics of Marriage Alliance

The most elementary benefit to be sought from a marriage alliance is peace with a group who without it are potential enemies. As far apart as northern Nigeria and the highlands of New Guinea, and no doubt in many places in between, people equate affines (or potential affines) with enemies. A Mambila, of a tribe on the Nigeria–Cameroun border, asked by an anthropologist who their traditional enemies were, would say: 'The men of X village, for we marry their daughters and they marry ours.' The anthropologist[2] interpreted this as indicating that marriages give rise to quarrels between affines, as indeed they do. But they are also ways of ending hostilities and some sort of guarantee against a renewal. In New Guinea, where the phrase 'We marry the people we fight' is current, it was true until fairly recently that a hitch in marriage negotiations or a failure to meet an affinal obligation could be a matter for a fight. This is most liable to happen if one or other of a betrothed couple backs out; either may do so, and in New Guinea a girl often does. She may do this at the moment when the bridegroom's kin are assembled at her home, and she is asked, on the last of several occasions, to say publicly that she agrees to the marriage. If she refuses there may be a free fight on the spot. If a

2. C. K. Meek, *Tribal Studies in Northern Nigeria*, 1931, Vol. 1, p. 533.

young man jilts a girl she may let it be known that she has bewitched him in revenge. This is a wrong for which her kin should pay compensation; if they refuse, the man's kin will attack them. Or she can get her kin to attack the faithless lover. If a girl jilts a man he may try to kill her, and there will certainly be a fight if he succeeds.

Nevertheless, if a marriage is successfully concluded, it does at least make possible the maintenance of 'intermittently peaceful relations'.[3] The reason for concluding particular marriages, apart from the wishes of the couple, which have more influence here than in many societies, is the desire of every small lineage to extend as widely as possible its network of partners in the ceremonial exchanges through which there is so much prestige to be gained.

Several writers on Arab peoples have shown how the game may be played where the rule is that a woman's closest agnate has the first claim on her, and that no one should open negotiations for a marriage without making sure that no nearer relative wants to assert his claim. It should be noted that the rules apply to first marriages only, and that many of these end in divorce, after which the partners can remarry with a much freer choice. A senior man in a Humr camp said to an unsatisfactory son-in-law: 'I didn't give you the girl because of your good character, I gave her to you because you are our brother.' In the same camp lived a young man called Ali whose father actually was of another lineage; his mother had come home when she was widowed, bringing with her a dozen cattle that were his inheritance – a large number for one man to own. Ali's agnatic kin could have got him back with his cattle by a marriage with one of their girls according to the rules, but his mother's brother planned to steal a march on them by marrying his daughter to Ali. Keeping the cattle together, an argument for the rule of marriage between agnates, was here an argument for disregarding the rules. Marriage within the *surra*[4] has the advantage for ordinary people that the payment demanded

3. M. J. Meggitt, op. cit., p. 128.
4. See above p. 44.

by the girl's mother is less and some of the feasting can be dispensed with. But important men are interested in allies outside. Thus the *omda* (officially recognized headman) of a division of the Humr, who was also the leader and richest man in his own camp, married his half-sister to an influential man outside whom he hoped to conciliate by the favour; and this although a member of the camp was backing two candidates for her, and was so angry that he split off from the camp taking his closest agnates with him.[5]

Emanuel Marx[6] has worked out in detail the marriage strategy of one division of the Zullam tribe of Bedouin in the Negev. The division is what he calls a 'co-liable group', a large lineage tracing descent (or supposed descent) for five generations or more, the members of which are jointly liable to pay compensation for any injury done by one of them to an outsider. Such a group is divided into sections, small lineages the members of which decide jointly on the marriages of their offspring. A section generally consists of a group of brothers with or without a father living, so that marriages of first cousins are marriages within the section; it is easy to see how they can be arranged and imposed, since the parents of both parties are jointly concerned in the marriage of each. Marriageable persons for whom no cousin is available are like trump cards to be played with careful consideration. One way of disposing of them is to maintain a single link with each other section in the co-liable group. When a link is broken by death or divorce it is renewed as soon as possible. But the makers of marriages also have to consider the economic advantages they may bring. One such advantage is access to water supplies in territory outside that of one's own group. Sections whose grazing areas are on higher ground need to be able to pasture their herds in the plains where the spring growth comes earlier. They also like to maintain links along the smuggling routes. But since the first priority is considered to be the linking of sections within the co-liable group, a given section may have only a few 'marriages to spare' for such wider alliances.

5. I. G. Cunnison, op. cit., pp. 56ff.
6. E. Marx, op. cit., Chapter 5.

Even the Gidjingali hunting bands[7] could turn 'spare marriages' to advantage. In a community of about a hundred adults where Hiatt made detailed records, half the women had reached puberty, when they were expected to marry as soon as possible, at times when there were no adult unmarried men with rights to them. This situation could of course be foreseen some years in advance. So the girl's guardians (mother and mother's brother) could promise her to some man who would then be expected to send them regular presents and be on their side in quarrels; and no doubt some men were better providers and better partisans than others.

Where there are no rules giving particular men a claim on particular women as brides, those who have daughters to bestow or sons to marry consider the advantages of an alliance with a particular lineage; at the very least, if their choice is limited, they will rule out a lineage that they consider has serious disadvantages. The question may be a narrower one: who is a desirable father-in-law, who a desirable son-in-law?

In a society with few differences of wealth and status, many people simply seek brides and accept bridegrooms who have nothing against them; one would expect that at that level the choice of the couple might be allowed greater weight, and in some cases this is certainly so. But even in such societies there may be individuals whose status and wealth makes them especially welcome as affines. Among the Taita of Kenya[8] such men are the elders who together keep the peace among their juniors by mediating in disputes, and discuss and take decisions in local affairs, mainly in matters of the performance of ritual. A man is normally married long before he reaches elderhood, so this is the moment to remind the reader again that although, for the sake of simplicity, generalizations about marriage are commonly made with the first marriage of both partners in mind, most African societies and many others permit a man to be married to more than one wife at a time. An elder, then, is typically a

7. See Chapter 3.
8. Grace Harris, 'Taita Bridewealth and Affinal Relations', in *Marriage in Tribal Societies*, ed. M. Fortes, 1962.

man already married who seeks an additional alliance; and naturally he seeks it on his own behalf, since he has long since become emancipated from his father's authority. He is also a man with more than average wealth in cattle; otherwise he could not have become an elder. All men with large herds, but elders particularly, use their cattle to make advantageous transactions. They put others in their debt by making loans in times of difficulty. They invite friends in distant neighbourhoods to look after some of their cattle. This is an insurance against losing the whole herd by disease; it is also a convenient way of concealing the possession of cattle on whom others might make claims. It is not a one-way arrangement; A has some stock herded with B, and B with A. Both can say of the whole herd, 'But only some of these beasts are mine.' In another kind of cattle partnership two men agree to supply one another with animals needed to make sacrifices or pay debts at times when it is inconvenient to take beasts from one or other herd. Elders make these arrangements both inside and outside their own locality, and outside it they are sometimes capped by a pact of blood-brotherhood which gives a man a sort of naturalization in his blood-brother's community. He may be expected to offer such arrangements to the father or brother of the girl he wants to marry, and he is likely to seek the daughters of men in the same position as himself, who also, having built up at home in their earlier years a network of relationships of mutual aid, are now seeking to extend this further. There is a parallel between this building up of partnerships for practical convenience and the New Guinea building up of exchange relationships which, even though they are focused on the great ceremonial exchanges of gifts, also have a utilitarian side. Out of such relationships comes also political importance. Men who have affinal links in distant localities can use their influence on behalf of fellow-villagers, who owe them support in return. They are called on to mediate in disputes and can stimulate and lead practical co-operation between villages.

Where there is room for wide differences in the amount of bridewealth to be agreed upon, a man must find a wife whose guardians will not demand more than he can give, a problem that is more acute when the payment is made in cash. People may think they know how many cattle their neighbours have, but nobody knows how much cash another man has, or, what is even more important, what other purposes he may have for it besides making marriage payments. For marriage negotiations to break down on this point would be humiliating to the bridegroom's kin, and the risk is avoided by making discreet inquiries before they are opened. Where the role of marriage broker is recognized this is one of his responsibilities. One consideration here, which weighs both with the Taita and another East African people, the Gisu of eastern Uganda, is that a son-in-law is expected, as an expression of the deference he owes his father-in-law, and his gratitude for the inestimable gift of a wife, to be willing to do small services whenever he is called upon. In one Gisu example a son-in-law bicycled 17 miles to buy nails for his father-in-law's new house. If you marry a girl whose home is far enough away, you will be out of reach of such demands. But her father will foresee this and exact a higher bridewealth, or expect it to be paid all at once. This is an additional reason why only men of wealth and status above average marry wives from a distance.

In Africa today there are still cattle herdsmen in remote areas whose life, including their marriages, is built on their stock. But in the greater part of the continent people are accustomed to earning cash incomes, even if these may seem sometimes pitiably small, and regard as influential affines people who can help them to profitable employment. Young men deliberately choose such affines; they are not forced by scheming parents to forego romantic unions. But the first step towards lucrative employment (apart from paid posts in political parties) is one that cannot be made through the influence of one's affines; it consists in going to school and staying right through the course. Hence today the educated constitute what is for practical purposes an endogamous class. They marry one another's sisters, and are not concerned with such matters as the distance between their homes, as they are likely to be employed away from home in any case. Within this class the bridewealth demanded among the Gisu is three times the average, and elaborate weddings are expected as well. The amount demanded is what an educated man's income is expected to bear; and the effect of the demand is that only a man with such an income can seek a wife in the educated class. The members of this class have of course also adopted a style of living alien to that of the rest of Gisu society, so that marriage outside it would create embarrassing situations for both parties.

Another region where people are expected to marry their cross-cousins – or rather, as we have seen it should be put, where a woman should give her children as marriage partners to the children of her brother – is southern India and Ceylon. Here much importance is attached to the duty of kinsmen to co-operate in all circumstances, and marriage between cousins is for that reason regarded as a surer alliance than one with outsiders. Yet the latter type is often chosen, and not in this case because there is no available cousin for a young person to marry. One reason again is difference in income. A man who has risen in the world may forget his kinsmen and prefer the company of others who live at his own new standard. (This can happen without any great diversity; the Nyoro of Uganda have a proverb, 'Your brother's wealth is no good to you.')

The Kandyan Sinhalese balance the principle that those who are already kin should marry against the principle that those who marry should be equals. This allows social climbers to reject their cousins as spouses – though not without making themselves unpopular. It also allows men to seek for their daughters husbands of slightly higher status than their own. Relative status is carefully calculated in terms of caste ranking, wealth, and, more recently, education; and in the final analysis equality can be attained by a dowry payment which is held to put husband and wife on an equal footing. The greater the recognized inequality, the greater the dowry; and of course beyond a certain point the inequality would be considered too great for any dowry to make it up.

Hypergamy

This is the prototype of the commonest of all marriage stra-
tegies. It has attracted particular attention in India because
it appears to contradict the principle of caste endogamy.
Despite the assumptions that are often made about strict
endogamy, it is actually the rule in northern India among the
higher castes that a woman should, if possible, marry into a
social stratum slightly higher than that into which she was
born. This is likely to be a higher subdivision of her own
caste. The divisions which intermarry in this way are formally recognized. Men say: 'We give girls to . . . We take
girls from . . .' The corollary of this attitude is the phrase
'We wouldn't give our daughters to . . .', a way of expressing
group superiority that has echoes in many parts of the world.
Obviously there can be no form of exchange here; there is a
one-way upward movement of women, and so of the children, who take their father's status since this is not a form of
marriage outside the group which is disapproved.

The rule does not, of course, hold good throughout the
society from the lowest to the highest. There are lines which
cannot be crossed, and so there are men who cannot marry
below them. If many fathers succeed in 'marrying up' their
daughters these men will be left without wives; while at the
top there will be women who must be content to marry their
equals, and perhaps can find no husbands if too many of
these equals have taken wives from the level below. But this
problem can be solved by polygyny.

The ideology of Indian marriage is that it is a ritual gift
demanding no return; it confers merit on both giver and
receiver. It is the fathers of girls, therefore, who take the
initiative in offering their daughters. Of course they make
careful inquiries about the families whom they might approach; the father of a nubile girl is expected to spend most
of his time in this way. He gives the girl a dowry, not as a
prestation to her father-in-law, but because it is her right; it
compensates her for the fact that she is entitled to no inheritance. 'Girls do not inherit, but to them, their husbands,

their children, we make gifts.'[9] But whatever may be said about a gift made without any question of return, the higher-ranking family are perfectly well aware that the return they make is the elevation of the children of the marriage to their level, and they can calculate what this is worth to them in payment of dowry. A hypergamous marriage, as this is called, is an exchange of status for wealth. As Kandyan Sinhalese succinctly put it: 'Women go up with dowry.' It is the prestige they expect to derive from the connection that leads Indians to get into debt when marrying their daughters, in the way that so much distressed British administrators for so long. A few years ago it was estimated that in the United Provinces one quarter of all outstanding debts had been incurred in the contraction of marriages. The (relatively) new kind of prestige conferred by an educated husband would also be thought worth the offer of a large dowry.

Material advantages too are expected from the outlay. A man with a well-connected daughter could expect better dowries to be offered at the marriage of his sons, and one really distinguished connection could enable him to marry other daughters advantageously, but without offering as high a dowry as he had for the first. And, in later years, when her brothers' children were growing up, a woman with a rich husband might be able to return some of the gifts made to her by helping them.

Hypergamy without any caste system can be seen in many peoples of the world. In a Greek village a father has two aims: to marry his daughters well and to make the most of his resources in land. To achieve the former aim he must find sons-in-law with work in a town – not necessarily important or very profitable work; they may be artisans, shopkeepers or clerks. To achieve the latter he must equip his sons by schooling for a town occupation, all but the one who is to stay at home and carry on the farm. Here the question is not so much of alliance with a higher-ranked family. The dowry

9. Statement quoted by L. Dumont, *Contributions to Indian Sociology*, IX, 1966, p. 110.

is given in land or the cash value of land, and more land can be used in dowry if fewer sons have to get their living from it. A town husband knows his value and expects his wife to bring a higher dowry than she would to a farmer. There is enough competition for urban sons-in-law to cause an inflation of the amount expected, and one consequence is that instead of limiting what is given in dowry to the share due to a daughter in inheritance, a part of her brothers' patrimony must be sacrificed. But these brothers too can ask for higher dowries on the strength of town connections which may be expected to be useful to their children, particularly in finding them jobs in town. One consequence is that, as the cost of marriage goes up, and with it the time it takes to amass the dowry, the age of marriage gets higher.

One can see the exchange of money for rank much nearer home, during the centuries in which trade and industry came to replace land ownership as the principal source of wealth. The aristocracy retained their titles but lost their incomes, and married first into the gentry – the untitled landowners – and then 'into trade', and later still found their brides in America, all in attempts to restore the family fortunes. It is worth pointing out at this stage that it is not worth while thinking about hypergamy unless you start high enough up in the scale to have something to offer. In a caste society a man of very low caste who became rich could make a hypergamous marriage for his daughter only in the unlikely event that he made his money in a place where his original status was not known; and in an industrial stratified society only a man on the make would want to. This is one of many aspects of marriage strategy and procedure which concern only the upper levels of society. It has already been indicated that marriage prestations, though they are supposed to be binding on everyone, can often not be made by poorer men, and the following chapter will show how it may be possible for them to dispense with many of the marriage formalities that are theoretically necessary.

CHAPTER 6

MARRIAGE PROCEDURES

THERE are some societies in which it is possible to get married almost without any formalities at all, and some in which a marriage without formality is a permitted alternative for people who cannot afford the formalities or do not attach importance to them. As was indicated in the previous chapter, there is a correlation between the amount of formality and display and the importance of the alliance that is being created. There are also in some societies – but these are different ones – ways of circumventing parental choice and forcing the consent of elders to a marriage agreed on by a young couple.

Informal Marriages

It is possible for a marriage to be created and announced in one breath by the simple fact that a couple are seen to be eating together. This is what happens in the Trobriand Islands in the Pacific, as they were described by Malinowski in the first ethnographic account to clothe formal statements of rules with the reality of actual behaviour. Since a marriage is concluded in such a simple way, a couple can marry in defiance of parental opposition, though they cannot always stay married, for reasons which will be made clear.

The Trobrianders, like so many people already described, can claim their cross-cousins in marriage, and people of high rank are particularly anxious to do so, and may assert a claim by betrothing a couple while they are children. But for the most part a man's choice of partner is free, since he does not depend on his parents for any action to make the marriage valid. Young boys and girls are allowed complete sexual freedom, and choose their mates after a series of liaisons of longer or shorter duration. (The phrase 'trial marriage' was on everyone's lips at the time when, in 1929, Malinowski published *The Sexual Life of Savages*.) When a couple begin to be seen together in public it is recognized that they intend to marry, and the way for the girl's parents to signify approval is to ask the young man for small gifts; he should not take the initiative in approaching them. A formal exchange of prescribed gifts then begins with a presentation of food from the girl's father to the new couple, which is taken as signifying his consent. Later shell ornaments are given by the boy's father to the girl's relatives.

According to Trobriand ideas a couple are married as soon as they have eaten together at the home of the husband. But the girl can be forcibly brought back to her own home. And there is yet a stronger sanction. It is the custom of the matrilineal Trobrianders that men supply their sisters with food even after they are married, so that after harvest every man is carrying yams from his own garden to some other village than his own. If a girl's brothers refuse to do this her household has not enough to live on. So that a 'runaway marriage' has a chance, but no certainty, of forcing the parents' hand.

Among the Kandyan Sinhalese too it is possible to establish a marriage simply by setting up house. The first step is taken, however, not in the permanent village, but at the time of year when those who have not enough irrigated land for their subsistence go up and live on plots which they cultivate in the jungle. This is called *chena* cultivation, and the peasant word for marriage is 'taking a woman to the *chena*'. In fact the girl's mother is asked to let her go, and sometimes her bridegroom, if he can be called so where there is no wedding, takes a suit of clothes for her to her home; she puts these on and leaves her old ones to her unmarried sisters. It will be remembered that they are expected to marry their cross-cousins, and that the same word is used for 'cross-cousin' and 'husband'. Sexual relations are permitted between cross-cousins, and they may be already living in the same house, so that the step to marriage and departure to the jungle plot is an almost imperceptible one. The one formality that is required is that if the girl is not marrying a first cousin she must ask the consent of a man in that relationship as her last act before she leaves home. Under British rule an attempt was made to establish the registration of marriages so as to distinguish between legitimate and illegitimate children, and there are registrars in every village; but people do not register marriages, though they do the birth of children, when they must name a father. The people who make formal, expensive marriages are the well-to-do and those who marry outside the kinship circle – usually the same category.

Preliminaries to Marriage

Although there are these exceptional cases, anthropologists embarking on a study commonly expect to find three stages – courtship, betrothal, marriage. The first, however, will be missing where marriage arrangements are in the hands of the older generation. There are good reasons, of various kinds, why a betrothal should be formalized some time before the ceremony of marriage. At the very least this requires some time to prepare; resources have to be mustered for the wedding feast, and where bridewealth is to be paid this may have to be got together by contributions from kin and loans from friends. But in a system of arranged marriages, betrothal may be made years before there is any question of concluding the marriage. A betrothal, as has been remarked, is a way of giving notice that a girl is reserved for a particular man, and notice may be given with greater or less formality. The betrothal period, especially in a marriage agreed on after courtship, also enables the future affines to develop their acquaintance.

There can be no courtship in the ordinary sense where marriages are entirely arranged by the elders of the couple. But, unless their union is determined in advance in a system where kinsmen have special claims, or by the bestowal of children as marriage partners by their guardians, there is still some need for preliminary negotiation. Where young people have no freedom of choice and no opportunities of meeting, these negotiations are made by a matchmaker, sometimes a professional, sometimes a man who is both clansman of the bridegroom and cognate of the bride. Such a person is often expected to report on the character of a prospective marriage partner and the circumstances of his or her family, and if the side that has taken the initiative in proposing the match has second thoughts, he can make this known without giving the offence that would be caused if the two fathers had been negotiating face to face. Matchmakers are particularly necessary in caste societies, where it is important to be satisfied that there is nothing discreditable in the ancestry of the prospective partners. Another explanation of the need for a neutral go-between is given in a different context by Fortes, who says of the Tallensi of northern Ghana that he is required because the marriage negotiations are conducted in the idiom of a struggle between enemies.

The possibility of courtship depends both on the absence of rules committing girls to a particular marriage and on the extent to which they are kept under their parents' control. In most African societies there were traditionally many opportunities for it, in particular at the dances that are the principal amusement of young people. Young men display their agility, sometimes for the benefit of a particular girl, and when the dancing is over couples disappear into the bush. Those African peoples among whom girls are not betrothed before puberty permit limited sex relations between adolescents, and these may even be formally recognized by a gift from the boy to the girl's father, as among the south-eastern Bantu. Here the girls used to be periodically examined by the old women to see whether they had been deflowered. But in general what is seriously disapproved in Africa is not the loss of virginity, but the bearing of children in circumstances not socially authorized. I use this phrase because the most serious sexual offence is not always held to be the bearing of children without legal marriage. This is sometimes severely punished, as among the Xhosa of South Africa, where an unmarried mother is disqualified from marriage, but such a rule is rare, and one may contrast with it the attitude of the Kipsigis in Kenya, who are not much disturbed by pregnancy before marriage, but consider it so dreadful for a girl to bear a child before she has been through her puberty ceremonies that in the old days, they say, they would have put her and her child to death.

Courtship in public, and subject to strict rules, may be allowed in societies where girls are closely guarded. This is what happens in rural Spain. There young men choose their girls at the Sunday evening promenade where all the unmarried people of the village circulate together. The suitor first walks with his girl in the promenade, then goes with her to the corner of her street and finally commits himself by asking to enter her house. He may go on making formal visits there for as much as ten years before they are married.

The most usual marriage procedure everywhere is a formal betrothal, preceded by negotiations of some kind, whether between the partners or their guardians, and followed by a formal public inauguration of the union. I have mentioned cases where this can be dispensed with and will mention more where it can be evaded.

Choice in Marriage

In Africa a betrothal ceremony commonly includes a formal expression by the girl of her acceptance of her husband. This could be taken to imply that any girl could refuse an unwanted partner, but when one thinks that this occasion must be the culmination of weeks of discussion and parental pressure, and that the refusal would have to be made in public, it seems likely that it would be as difficult as it would be in England for a young woman to balk in church at the words 'I will'. The anthropologists who have described betrothal procedures do not mention cases where the girl has refused to make the appropriate gesture. They describe, rather, elopements and threatened – occasionally actual – suicides, parental beatings and sometimes parental yielding. An elopement often forces parental hands, for reasons which will be discussed later. Parental pressure is no doubt greatest where a particular marriage is considered especially important, and when no such question arises it must often happen that parents have no objection to a suitor who has already approached their daughter. Evans-Pritchard, writing of the Nuer, among whom courtship is freely allowed, remarks that a girl knows her prospective husband well before she goes to him in marriage and that she has plenty of time to withdraw between betrothal and consummation. 'I do not say that pressure may not be put on her by her family to accept her husband, but Nuer girls are not easily coerced.'[1]

Evans-Pritchard's account of the Nuer gives one of the most detailed descriptions that we have of the series of ceremonies by which an African marriage is concluded. In this case there are three: betrothal, marriage and consummation, and the performance of each depends upon the delivery of a sufficient number of the bridewealth cattle. Once a marriage is agreed on, both sides want to see it concluded; so the bridegroom's press for dates to be fixed for the rituals and the bride's for more cattle to be handed over. The most striking part of the betrothal ceremony is the driving of the first instalment of the bridewealth cattle to the girl's home. Its religious element consists in the sacrifice of an ox to the ancestors, and the meat of the ox provides a feast which is cooked by the bride's people and eaten by the bridegroom's. From this time on the couple are spoken of as husband and wife, and the man adopts the formal behaviour required from a son-in-law to his affines. At the wedding the negotiations on bridewealth are finally concluded, the ancestors are called on to witness the marriage, and the young men dance all night. But the bride has still never been to her husband's home. It is at the consummation ceremony that he asks her mother for permission to take her away, giving her small presents in return. The consummation takes place at his village; the entry on a sexual relationship sanctioned by marriage is symbolized by a pretence of reluctance by the bride, who actually is rarely a virgin. 'Maidenhood', as

1. E. E. Evans-Pritchard, op. cit., p. 95.

Evans-Pritchard comments, 'is a social, not a physical, state.'
It is after this that the man is entitled to damages for adultery; so we might say that he becomes a son-in-law before
becoming a husband. After this there is another sacrifice to
the ancestors, who this time are asked to bless the marriage
with sons to continue the lineage. Then comes a rite
which is held to be an indispensable part of the ritual, the
giving of bracelets by the girls who have come with the bride
to the kinsmen of the bridegroom. Finally the girl's head is
shaved and she takes off all her ornaments and receives new
ones from her husband's kin, an act symbolic of change of
status which closely parallels that of the informal Kandyan
marriage. She does not stay with her husband even now; but
this is a matter to be discussed later.

There seems to be no way for a Nuer girl to force unwilling parents to agree to her marriage with a lover. But
some of them do live with men of their choice to whom they
are not married. Usually these are women who have been
married, but have left their husbands for other men who
cannot or will not pay bridewealth.

Fortes' account of the Tallensi shows how the evasion of
formal rules of marriage negotiations can be something more
than an expedient for girls who do not like their father's
choice or boys who cannot raise their bridewealth cattle.
Elopement for them is a recognized, named procedure, not
an uncountenanced breach of rule. A girl who elopes must
have the connivance of someone in the household, her
mother or a brother, and her suitor buys this with gifts. It is
the father who must be hoodwinked, and Fortes sees the
process as a 'conspiracy of minors' – women and dependent
young men against the holder of authority. To agree to a
negotiated marriage is, for the suitor, to accept defeat in
advance.

But, as Fortes puts it, the real struggle begins only after
the elopement, and even if in fact the parents on both sides
have nothing against the match the transactions are 'conducted in the idiom of a struggle between hostile groups'.[2]

2. M. Fortes, *The Web of Kinship among the Tallensi*, 1949, p. 91.

('We marry those we fight' again.) If, however, the girl's father is not complaisant, 'he may use ritual pretexts, exploit ties of cognatic kinship with the abductors' lineage or clan, even, in extremity, threaten to kill himself on their doorstep, or in the old days to stir up war against their clan'. The young man hides the girl, and his elders support him as a matter of prestige. A gift known as the placation gift – which is required in a negotiated marriage also – is eventually sent. This, Fortes says, marks the truce, but even when the first bridewealth cow has been paid, there is no more than a 'promise' of peace.

A Taita (southern Kenya) couple already betrothed may elope if they are tired of waiting for the girl's parents to be satisfied with the bridewealth they have received. Here the required betrothal gifts include one of money to the girl as a return for her consent, and by accepting this she is held to commit herself to elope if her suitor asks her. He may stage an abduction, in which case the girl puts up a show of resistance. The situation is described by Grace Harris in terms that would equally apply to a Trobriand marriage without consent: the couple behave as spouses and the question is whether they will be allowed to live as spouses. The girl's father tries to get her back, but he knows that if she has run away once she is likely to again. He has no such weapon as the Trobriander has; he can refuse to regard the marriage as legal, but he cannot starve the couple out. So he puts on a show of indignation and accepts a promise of bridewealth. But it is the father who has lost the game; the husband has gained credit by as much as he would otherwise have had to wait before taking his bride home. Christian parents are in a special difficulty. For them what makes the marriage irrevocable is the church wedding, so they are anxious not to allow this until they are sure of the bridewealth. But if their daughter elopes they have to choose between seeing her live in sin and risking the bridegroom's default.[3]

Gisu too have their ways of beating the system. A Gisu

3. G. Harris, 'Taita Bridewealth and Affinal Relationships', in M. Fortes, ed. *Marriage in Tribal Societies*, 1962, p. 68.

couple who elope go to the man's maternal uncle, who, as a non-member of either of the lineages in confrontation, can act as mediator and persuade the girl's father to enter on bridewealth discussions. As with the Tallensi, the boy's side score by the elopement, which is a demonstration of strength, and the boy himself will find he can assert his independence against later demands from his father-in-law. Or he may make his sweetheart pregnant, and then it is not he but the girl's father who is faced with a shot-gun wedding. But this method is not well thought of, because it is held to be ritually dangerous for a girl to become pregnant in her own home, and also for the bridewealth discussions to begin before the child is born; and Gisu consider it a disgrace to both parents for a child to be born before marriage. If it is the boy's family who oppose the marriage, he may take cattle without permission and present them to the girl's father, who can then notify the boy's family that the marriage has been concluded. This proceeding puts both fathers in an awkward position. The boy's father is likely to be criticized for his meanness in refusing to give him the cattle, and he will also have to compensate any of his kin from whom the boy has taken beasts. The girl's father has connived at an irregular match; this will make him unpopular with those who should have had a say in it, both his own kin and the boy's, and although the son-in-law is the gainer by this, he will not give his father-in-law the deference normally due to a senior affine. Only after an elopement is it easy to establish friendly relations.[4]

In this respect their neighbours across the Kenya border, the Vugusu, make an interesting contrast. Here it is marriage after an elopement that is likely to produce lasting ill-feeling between affines. As with the Tallensi an elopement can be a deliberate assertion of defiance, not made necessary either because the girl's parents refuse consent or because the man cannot produce the cattle, and it is particularly common when a polygynist marries a second or further

4. J. La Fontaine, 'Gisu Marriage and Affinal Relations', in *Marriage in Tribal Societies*, pp. 102–3.

wife. But if it is a way of avoiding the bridewealth payment the girl will have to hide somewhere from her angry brothers, who are in danger of losing the cattle one of them would marry with.

Abductions, on the other hand, are arranged by collusion with fathers who cannot manage to provide a wedding feast. 'Why don't you come and fetch her if you are in such a hurry?' a father may say, pretending to be joking. Since in this case he does not want the girl back, the rest of the marriage procedure is gone through in the normal way.

Elopement is indeed a way of escape in many African societies, and if it does not often cause a father to relent at once, it may lead other members of the community to put pressure on him. But there are other ways for a youth or a girl to assert their own choice. A Zulu girl could go to the home of the man she wanted to marry, and might sometimes be put up to this by a father anxious for a particular match; it seems that her request could not be refused. A Kipsigis boy could secure a girl for himself by performing a piece of the marriage ritual which could not be done more than once for any girl – catching her as she came from her puberty ceremony and tying a grass bracelet on her wrist. Vugusu girls are said in the past to have been able to make their choice at the conclusion of the young men's initiation, but usually this was just another way for a couple who already had an understanding to forestall their parents' choice.

A girl could sometimes refuse to do some ritual action that was considered an essential part of the marriage ceremony: to wear the ornaments that marked her as a bride, for example. Or she could render the marriage impossible by breaking one of the taboos associated with it: for example to drink milk from one of her own marriage cattle. This was a possible course for a Vugusu girl; she might also try to drive the marriage cattle back to the bridegroom's homestead. Her lover would encourage her by going with his friends to sing songs making fun of the bridegroom where she could hear them as she worked in the fields.

For a long time now there have also been two new-style

T–D

ways of escape: a civil marriage, which is not easy unless you are in town, and escape to town with the idea of getting married later.

Bemba and Nyakyusa Marriage Procedure

For patrilineal peoples with bridewealth marriage, the betrothal of children is a way of staking out a claim – announcing that a girl is reserved, as it has already been put. But in some matrilineal societies such a betrothal is the beginning of a continuous process that culminates in the union as soon as the girl has been through her puberty ceremony. The one in which this process was first described is the Bemba of Zambia, and the account of it by Dr Audrey Richards is one of the fullest that we have. Although young Bemba girls, like many others in Africa, may be married to much older men, the procedure that she describes as typical of Bemba tradition presupposes that both parties are young when it begins. And although girls may be given in marriage by their elders, at the time when Dr Richards was in Bemba country (1930–34) quite young children chose one another as partners. The youth sent a small present – at that time sixpence – to the girl's father, and its acceptance marked the betrothal. He then invited the girl to visit him; she went with a band of her age-mates and they spent the night in talk and jesting with him and his friends. This was not a visit for sexual purposes; on the contrary, the girl was expected to keep in the background and the couple were never alone together. Moreover, it would seem from other parts of the account that the boy too might be quite young at this stage, since we are told that when he moved to the girl's village he would be about fifteen.

As with other matrilineal peoples the couple were expected to make their home in the village of the girl's mother; this move was the first step towards it. The youth now began to work for her father, particularly in the arduous business of climbing trees and lopping the branches, to be burnt on the ground where they fall and fertilize it with the ashes. He might do this for two or three years, depending partly on the age of his bride. During this time her parents symbolized their acceptance of him as one of their community by giving him presents of food, beginning with an elaborate feast cooked in his village. The girl would take on small domestic tasks, such as sweeping his hut and fetching water, and later would sleep with him, not necessarily having full intercourse. When she seemed to be approaching first menstruation she would be brought home lest she should conceive before the puberty ceremony – initiation, as it is generally called – the holding of which both permitted and blessed the bearing of children. This could not be strictly called a marriage ceremony, since it had to be performed for every girl, and some were not betrothed when they came to the age for it. But for a betrothed girl it was the most important ritual of her marriage, and the bridegroom both made payments to her parents and to the woman in charge of the ritual and had his part in it, being required to go with her into the hut where the initiands were shown a number of pottery images each symbolizing some aspect of married life. He had to bring with him presents representing his contribution to the new household (salt, meat, firewood), and the bow and arrow with which he would shoot game *and also* 'protect his wife against adulterers'. One might guess that the idea was rather to shoot the adulterer after the event, but in any case the point had now been reached when adultery with his wife would be an infringement of his rights. This was followed as soon as possible by the consummation ceremony, which initiated a ritual of purification after intercourse that the couple were expected to continue through their married life. The bride was given a tiny pot, 'the marriage pot', from which the water would be taken to wash their hands, a ritual which distinguished marital from extra-marital intercourse.[5]

It is worth mentioning the unusual case of the Nyakyusa in Tanzania, who reckon descent in the male line and marry

5. A. I. Richards, *Bemba Marriage and Present Economic Conditions*, 1940, pp. 61–5.

with bridewealth, but also betroth girls as children and combine puberty rituals with marriage. Monica Wilson describes the relationship of such a girl with her future husband: 'The view of most Nyakyusa is that a girl should become accustomed to her husband gradually and that it is good for her to visit him from time to time, sweeping his house, cleaning the byre, drawing water and cooking for him, and learning the act of love-making with him and no one else.'[6] Anthropologists are warned to avoid guessing about 'influences', but one may just note that the home of the Nyakyusa is on the edge of the 'matrilineal belt' which stretches from Malawi and Zambia across the Congo; and one anthropologist, more prone to conjecture than the rest, believes that their patrilineal chiefs were immigrants from the Great Lakes.[7]

The Crucial Validating Act

Nearly all marriage procedures involve both transfers of goods and the performance of ritual – if one leaves out the wholly secular modes of contracting marriage that are available in industrialized societies; and even they are called in France, where they were first introduced, civil *rites*. But the essential act to make the marriage valid may be one or the other. In a Christian marriage the priest declares a couple to be man and wife when they have exchanged the requisite vows, and they become legally married by signing the marriage register. The significance of the bridewealth transfer in Africa has been discussed at length. In Japan the couple reach the point of no return when the groom's family make a gift of cash to the bride's as a contribution to the wedding expenses. In rural China before the Revolution it was the betrothal ceremony itself that was binding; in Islam the dower gift from husband to wife or the signing of a contract.

The crucial acts in a Hindu marriage are ritual. The details of ritual vary considerably from place to place, but

6. M. Wilson, *Rituals of Kinship among the Nyakyusa*, 1957, p. 86.
7. M. Wilson, *The Oxford History of South Africa*, 1969, p. 17.

the essentials are the joining of the couple's hands and their walking, hands joined, round a ritual fire kindled by the Brahmin who presides over the ceremony and blesses the pair. The most important rite in southern India is the tying of an ornament – the *tali* – round the bride's neck by her husband. The Hindu Marriage Code enacted by Congress in 1955 disregards ritual and says that 'a man and a woman marry each other when both, having formed the irrevocable intention of living together ... signify this solemn determination in a public acknowledgement and announcement in conformity with law'; and an English commentator adds, 'The great notoriety which usually surrounds practically every wedding, and the inevitable entries in the genealogists' books in the case of a family of any standing, secure that the factum and date of nearly every marriage will not be disputed.'[8] In the eyes of the small society to which the couple belong it is certainly the general publicity rather than the performance of specific acts that causes their new status to be recognized. It would of course be inconceivable for a formal wedding to omit the crucial rites, but it would be equally inconceivable for anyone to try to have a quiet wedding by performing the rites out of their accepted context of ceremonial, feasting and display.

Only one account of Indian marriage procedures mentions a secular legalizing element comparable to African bridewealth payment. This is the very detailed account by M. N. Srinivas of the Coorgs in south India, on the borders of Mysore, who have a number of local customs different from those of high-caste Hindus. Here the marriage ceremony includes an exchange of set speeches between the representatives of the bride's and bridegroom's families. The former asks whether the bride will be given a share in every kind of property of her husband's joint family and is told that she will. He then publicly states what property is going with the bride from her joint family. He gives the groom's representative 'twelve pieces of gold'. Actually he gives eleven pebbles; these stand for the rights in her own joint family

8. D. J. Derrett, *Introduction to Modern Hindu Law*, 1963.

that the bride is giving up – only eleven-twelfths because they are not casting her off altogether. The dominant idea here is not the legal rights acquired by the husband but the property rights given up by the wife. The pebble that is not given signifies her right to go home if her marriage breaks up. Divorce is called 'giving up the pebbles', but the pebbles go with the bride; they are not exchanged for her. If there is any buying it is she who buys her way into her husband's joint family. This is the step that must be formally undone if a wife is divorced or a widow remarried. These possibilities too are covered by the set speeches. When the husband's representative has received the pebbles, he asks who will be 'responsible for telling her what is right and repairing the wrong' if she runs home with some complaint – and the possibilities are enumerated, as are the types of property – and the bride's representative says that he will. And he in his turn asks who will be responsible for sending her home, 'with servants for company and torches for the road', if she 'comes upon misfortune' – i.e. is divorced or widowed. This will be the responsibility of the husband's representative, and the two exchange 'witness-money' in token of their undertakings. These men are friends, not members, of the respective joint families.

In most Indian marriages there are a series of feasts; first the two sides make their feast separately, each in his own village, and then there is a joint one when the bridegroom arrives for the wedding. He comes with a procession of his friends, transported in bullock-carts, or nowadays cars and buses, and accompanied by music, which the lower-caste members of his village provide. For his family this is the major expense of the wedding, but the bride's family must provide the feast of welcome, and they may find themselves involved in more expense than they bargained for, so it is usual for the numbers to be agreed on in advance. You honour your bride's family by bringing many guests, but you can insult them by bringing more than they expected, so that they have to send out for more food. But after the wedding the bride goes home again and is later brought in procession to her husband's house, so that is their time to get their own back. There are elaborate rules for the giving of gifts, not only between affines but within the groups of kin on both sides. In accordance with the principle that marriage is a gift of the bride to be followed by other gifts, the bride's close agnates make gifts both to the groom and to his agnates. But on each side the fathers receive gifts from their own kin to help pay their wedding expenses; a careful account is kept of these, and they are reciprocated at later weddings.

The relatives of both spouses' mothers make gifts of cloth not to the couple but to their parents and siblings. These are carried round the village on a brass tray in a procession with a drummer at its head. A great number of kin contribute to these, and also affines of siblings of the spouse who are already married. Indeed, this is an occasion for people already linked in affinity to recognize their relationship by gift-giving.

The aim of this chapter has been to indicate what actions are held to be indispensable to make a marriage valid in societies where the memory of a public event, and not a written record, is the essential evidence that it has been duly created. Most of these actions have a symbolic character; the most widely found symbols will be discussed in the next chapter.

CHAPTER 7

THE SYMBOLISM OF MARRIAGE RITUAL

DETAILED descriptions of marriage ritual are of little significance in themselves. In a good ethnographic monograph such a description places the rites in their context. It shows how the actions that different participants are required to perform express their present relationship, or the one that is being created, to the bride and bridegroom and their kin. It shows how objects and acts are common to marriage and other rites of a single society and thus interprets their symbolism. And the analysis may be extended to cover their whole symbolic system.

In a general discussion one cannot and should not attempt to trace out in detail the elaborate series of ritual acts that accompany marriage in even one society. We should rather examine the features common to many marriage rites. Since the social process that they express and confirm has certain nearly universal features, and many more that are common to peoples of similar social structure, we should expect to find similarities in the mode of expression.

The Ritual of Passage

Van Gennep, the French sociologist who was a contemporary though not a follower of Durkheim, identified a type of ritual to be found in every society which he called 'the ritual of passage' ('*rite de passage*'): ritual which accompanies and symbolizes some change of time, of place, of social status. It is the last type that has most interested anthropologists. We now sometimes call it the life crisis ritual. Van Gennep noted that passage rituals mark those changes of status that every individual goes through in the course of a normal life. At birth a naming or 'showing' ceremony marks his acceptance as a social being; at puberty he passes from the status of child to adult; at marriage he becomes a potential parent and household head, and a whole realignment of relations is created by new ties of affinity; at death he becomes an ancestor, and again the alignment of relations among the living is changed when his successor steps into his place. All these rituals take the same form: the separation of a person from others of the category he is leaving, a 'marginal' period when he is in a sort of limbo (a dangerous condition), and his re-admission to society in his new status.

This is Van Gennep's formula. It may not be possible always to identify all his three stages, but it is always illuminating to look for them. The other aspect of ritual consists in the fact that it is an appeal to some personalized being, however the object of cult is conceived in a given society, to bless the new status on which someone is entering; hence one must ask what aspects of this status are emphasized by symbolic treatment.

On the whole the passage of the bride from the status of maiden to wife is more emphasized in marriage ritual than the corresponding change in status of the man. In societies which practise initiation he will have already entered ritually upon adult status, perhaps a long time before if he has had to wait for bridewealth. And although adult status authorizes him to marry and beget children, it also has other and wider consequences for him. For a woman in these societies adult status signifies ripeness for wifehood and motherhood and nothing else. It is, then, common for a girl to go through a period of seclusion before her marriage and much less common to find anything corresponding for a man. Where a girl's marriage and puberty ceremonies are combined the separation period involves more or less elaborate series of rites performed by women in some place which men, and uninitiated children, are not allowed to approach. The initiation of two Bemba girls was witnessed by Audrey Richards in 1931, when the ritual was already beginning to be abandoned. It lasted a month; it was said that in the old days it would have been continued much longer. The girls lived during this time in a hut which had been cleared of all its contents. Some of the ritual was performed there and some in the bush. They had to enter the hut backwards 'to show,' said the Bemba, 'that they are leaving their old way of life'. They were covered with blankets and so concealed from view, as they were whenever they left the hut. Although the central figures in the ritual, they 'seemed to lose all personality for the observer',[1] a striking way of expressing their 'liminal' position between two statuses. In another part of Zambia, Ndembu country, a girl at her puberty-marriage rites has to lie covered with blankets, motionless for a whole day at the foot of a sacred tree, perhaps another expression of withdrawal of personality in the intermediate stage between child and wife.

The 'seclusion' period of a Nyakyusa girl, according to the traditional rites, was much less taxing, although it lasted longer. For her, seclusion implied neither solitude nor any withdrawal of personality, but for as much as three months she was 'separated' from the community in the sense that she did not take part in everyday occupations, but spent her time with younger girl companions and had to avoid being seen by men. She slept in her mother's hut on a litter of banana leaves, significant because throwing away these leaves was one of the ritual acts that marked the end of the marginal period and her emergence as a bride. Youths came to the hut at night for sex play with her and her attendants. In the daytime she wove mats which she would take with her to her new home. Although she could go out she did not work in the fields, so that this was the least physically strenuous time of her whole life, and she might expect to be plump and well at the end of it. It is not only the Nyakyusa who say that brides 'get fat' during their seclusion, and we must remember that where people never have more than enough to eat, getting fat is a matter of satisfaction, as it is not in affluent societies. But the idea that brides are 'fattened' like prize turkeys, and that this is the essence of the seclusion period, is a very great mistake.

1. A. I. Richards, *Chisungu*, 1956, p. 63.

For a Chinese bride, seclusion in the limbo of the transition period is a part of the actual transit from her own home to her husband's, a process that is everywhere accompanied by its own distinctive and usually elaborate ritual. She is heavily veiled and carried in a closed sedan chair, sometimes in a box inside it, from one house to the other, and if the distance between them is actually not long, she will be taken a roundabout way to make it appear so and to emphasize the change she is making. The actual physical barriers between her and the secular world may seem to be excessive in comparison with what is found elsewhere; the reason is the Chinese belief in the existence of evil influences of many kinds which might affect her, and through her her new family.

Where, as sometimes happens in Africa, the bride is secluded after she has gone to her husband and the marriage has been consummated, one can say that she is still held not to have fully become a wife, and that she enters on this status when she begins to do a woman's normal work in her new home. Real-life rituals cannot always be fitted into neat schemes of separation, marginality, re-integration, in logical order; all one can say is that these processes are symbolized in different parts of many ritual sequences.

Nyakyusa traditional ritual clearly expressed the casting off of an early status as the new one was entered. At the end of her stay in the seclusion hut the girl was washed all over with medicated water. The leaves on which she had slept were cleared out of the hut and burned, and she jumped over the fire (crossing a boundary). Her hair was shaved, another very common way of ending a ritual by casting something off.

Before a Hindu wedding both bride and bridegroom are ritually bathed with oil a number of times, and during these days they both stay at home and do not work. This too is a seclusion or separation rite which also has a beautifying effect, and it too ends with a casting off, this time of clothes which are replaced by new ones. At a high-class wedding among Kandyan Sinhalese one element of the ritual is the changing of the bride's clothes, and, as was mentioned earlier, this seems to have once been the only ritual act in an informally concluded marriage. The suitor would bring clothes to the girl, and she agreed to the marriage by accepting them. When she left her home she left her own clothes to her unmarried sisters. Leaving home in clothes given by her husband symbolized not only separation from her parents but becoming dependent on him instead of them.

Much marriage ritual, not excepting that in a Christian church, includes admonitions to one or other of the couple, or both, on their duties. This is also often a feature of puberty ritual, since preparation for adult life is held to be essentially preparation for marriage. The Bemba rites include dances imitating birds or animals from whose behaviour a girl should learn what to imitate or avoid. Of course they are told what the lesson is, but the pantomime, and the special circumstances of the performance, are supposed to impress it more than a mere homily would. Large numbers of pottery images, most of them symbolic rather than directly depicting the points being made, are displayed before the girls; the presentation of these objects as the revelation of a mystery again makes the teaching impressive. Nyakyusa girls are given explicit instruction in both sexual and domestic behaviour.

Many marriage rites include some kind of symbolic representation of a wife's domestic activities. When, for example, a Nuer bride finally goes to her husband's home – not until her first child is weaned – her parents give her a porridge spoon and a gourd to drink milk from.

Like the Sinhalese girl's new clothes, these objects symbolize her move to economic dependence on her husband, *also* the work she will do for him, since it is she who will hoe the grain and milk the cattle. Her parents give him the spoon and the gourd as they give him a domestic partner.

Since for men initiation ceremonies and marriage do not coincide, marriage ritual for them includes very much less symbolism of their marital duties, or indeed reference to them. Some boys' initiation procedures include instruction on such duties as part of the teaching on the responsibilities of adult life. Some do not. It has been mentioned that a Bemba husband, rather exceptionally, is shown, along with his bride, the secret pottery figures on which the girls' instruction is focused, and later he is urged to make big gardens at the same time as the girl is told to cook big meals. Here a part of the ritual is the formal teaching of both partners by their elder kinsmen and women, but it seems that this refers only to magical precautions to be observed during the wedding night.

Marriage marks an irreversible change of status; one may be widowed or divorced, but once married one has finally moved out of the ranks of the not-married. This is enough to make it a *rite de passage* in Van Gennep's sense. But it involves other crucial changes too. One or other partner, or both, moves away from the natal home to some other, and for a woman, though not to the same extent for a man, the new ties created by marriage must weaken those with her own parents and siblings. Only in those societies where a married woman continues to live in her own home is this not so.

The Transfer of the Bride

A large part of marriage ritual is concerned with a woman's change of residence and the partial severance of her links with her own kin. This would not have surprised Van Gennep, who saw rituals of change of place as a special category. But he did not give much consideration to the question of the tension between the old kin ties and the new. This is dramatized in many marriage rites, and symbolized without great emphasis in even more. Its minimal expression can be seen in the Christian church ritual where the bride enters the church on her father's arm, veiled (in the marginal state), and leaves it on her husband's, with the veil thrown back.

Rituals express in many ways the reluctance of the bride to leave her home, and of her kin to let her go. They often include weeping and lamentation, and this has been taken to show how cruelly wives expect to be treated in societies that

have not advanced to European standards. There is a grain
of truth in this; mothers-in-law are, as a rule, more severe
than mothers; young wives have to work harder than they
did as girls at home; sometimes they lose much freedom –
this depends on the degree of freedom they have in particular
societies. But the champions of oppressed womanhood have
not always realized how much the manifestations of grief and
reluctance are obligatory.

In patrilineal societies the formal transference of the bride
to her husband is the crucial and most publicized feature of
the ritual, even though, as a later chapter will show, it may
not mark the point at which the new household is actually
set up. Her husband's friends come to fetch her, as in the
Indian *barat*, or her own go out with her and meet her husband's party at a point between the two homes, as in parts of
East Africa. Such a meeting may be marked by a mock
battle; this is recorded of the ancient Greeks and Romans,
and was observed among some tribal Indian peoples, and by
early travellers in central Asia. It was even described as a
Welsh custom by Lord Kames in 1807, in one of our earliest
studies of custom. These observations gave rise to the nineteenth century theory of 'marriage by capture' as one of the
ways in which our remoter ancestors found themselves
brides. McLennan, who first discussed ritual captures, did
not always distinguish clearly between a simulated abduction
and a real elopement, but he did recognize that the wealth of
ethnographic examples was not evidence that any contemporary society regularly got wives by stealing them. His
explanation was that this aspect of marriage ritual commemorated a time in the past when they did, because, he
argued, nomad peoples first practised female infanticide because girl children were 'useless mouths' who merely im-
peded them on the march, and then had to steal wives
because of the shortage of women. In a later generation
W. H. R. Rivers offered an explanation in terms of cross-
cousin marriage. Cross-cousin marriage, as he rightly saw, is
an arrangement which 'gives certain persons a vested
interest' in the women of a related group, and conflicts as

part of marriage ritual, he suggested, recalled a past when a husband who sought to take a woman away from her cross-cousins had to do it by force.

Today we think, as I have indicated, that this part of marriage ritual, along with much else, simply underlines the separation of a girl from the kin among whom she has spent all her life, and her move to a home where she will arrive as an outsider and may have to work a hard passage before she is fully accepted as a member. She wants to be married, of course; she may love her new husband or have nothing against him; but she is going to a new parental authority, a new, perhaps unknown place, more responsibility than she has had to bear before, under the eyes of people disposed to be critical. Maurice Freedman, writing of the Chinese,[2] says that their marriage rites as a whole express the fear, or even the recognition, that the new wife brings danger with her as well as the blessings of progeny: danger because of the strains of any alliance, and because the children she bears will grow up into 'a new family pressing for the dissolution of the old'. He is interpreting them from the husband's point of view, but it may well be that we have not given enough attention to similarly ambivalent attitudes in the wife and her kin.

In any case, African marriage rites in many different ways express reluctance of the bride to go to her new home, which has to be overcome by the bridegroom and his friends. In the mock capture they overcome it by force, otherwise by gifts. 'How mercenary African girls are!' I used to hear missionaries say. 'They won't do anything without asking for payment.'

A classic description of the combination of the capture theme with this kind of mock bargaining is given by the missionary, Roscoe,[3] in his book on Ganda custom. In some cases, 'when the two parties met half-way, the bridegroom's friends scattered cowry shells [used by the Ganda as a kind of currency] and whilst the bride's party were picking

2. M. Freedman, *Rites and Duties*, 1967.
3. J. Roscoe, *The Baganda*, 1911.

them up, the other party carried off the bride, dropping shells as they ran and being chased by the bride's friends.' Later he tells how the bride on arrival at her husband's home would refuse to enter, then to sit down, to eat, and to go to bed, and be won over at each stage by a gift of cowry shells; 'this proceeding was thought to be a test of their mutual affection.' Among the peoples of Nyanza Province in Kenya, as they were described much later, the mock fight was one between girls; if the bridegroom's side were outnumbered the bride might even be taken home again. Of course this did not prevent the marriage, but it made the bridegroom's people look ridiculous. Wagner sees in the mock fight something more than an expression of reluctance to part with daughter, sister, playmate. It is a demand for respect for the bride in her new home – since a poor turn-out by the bridegroom's sisters is a failure in respect for which they can be put to shame; and it establishes her as someone who is not merely a tolerated outsider but has been fought for, just as the bridewealth shows that she is highly valued. In fact it is here a crucial part of the ritual, not in the sense that there could be no valid marriage without it, but in the sense that a wife may remind her husband in a quarrel that she didn't elope with him, but was properly captured.

As for the 'mercenary' demands, of course people who know they are entitled to a present will try to get the best one they can; this is part of the fun. But the fact that this procedure is essentially symbolic, prolonging and emphasizing the transfer period and the strength of the kin ties that are being partially broken, is perhaps best emphasized by the Indian song that is sung to welcome the new bride and refers to a completely imaginary and impossible bargain; also obliquely to the constant tension in a joint family household between the component individual families. The bride is supposed to say:

'O Mother-in-law . . . I will not get down from my palanquin
Unless you give me a separate fireplace.
O Father-in-law . . . I will not get down from my palanquin
Unless you build a separate big house for me.'

Oscar Lewis, from whom this song is quoted,[4] also gives the lamentations at their loss by the bride's kin whom she is leaving. One of these is a supposed dialogue between the bride and her father in which she asks who will do the household chores she is leaving behind; her reluctance to go is here ascribed to her by the women who are losing her. Another song calls on the procession to halt for something she has left behind – her playmates and her kin. The most striking of all in this context is sung while the couple walk seven times around the sacred fire. The first six couplets describe her as 'her grandfather's granddaughter' and so on, referring to closer and closer kin; the last Lewis translates as:

> 'Here she takes the seventh round
> And lo! the daughter becomes alien.'

The same theme of reluctance that must be overcome is shown in those marriage procedures in which the bride returns home, sometimes several times, immediately after her formal transfer to her husband, and alternatively in the custom that a bride takes with her to her new home a younger sister who may stay with her some time. Of course there are commonsense reasons why a newly married girl should like to keep in contact with her family and home; there is nothing magical in these procedures. But I include them in the behaviour symbolic of a reluctant transfer because they are prescribed actions; they are not something that the bride does of her individual choice. In a Chinese wedding it is a younger brother who accompanies her.

A more symbolic way of keeping in contact with home is that of the Logoli girl in Kenya, who takes her mother's sleeping-hide with her to sleep on all through her married life (except for the wedding night).

---

4. O. Lewis, *Village Life in Northern India*, p. 186.

Expressions of Hostility

Junod's description of the Tsonga betrothal visits,[5] made first from the boy's side and then from the girl's, could similarly be interpreted in terms of reluctance that has to be overcome. When the boys are invited to enter the bride's village they begin by refusing; later they refuse to put down the sticks and shields that they have brought as part of their finery, and the girls have to take these from them; and when mats are spread for them to sit on they stay standing, waiting to be entreated. When food is brought, again they first refuse it, and in one section of the Tsonga they demand payment before they will eat. The girls in this section, when they make the return visit, demand money gifts to enter the village, to move from the central square to the bridegroom's house, to enter his house, to sit down on the mats, to reply to the greetings of their hosts and to accept food.

This two-sided reluctance cannot well be explained in the same way as the mock capture, followed by placation in the form of gifts, that I have described earlier. Rather it expresses the attitude that I have quoted several times already: 'We marry those we fight.' A Tsonga marriage, like many others, links two lineages that could otherwise be openly hostile in an alliance that will always be uneasy, as each side suspects the other of falling short in its obligations, or sides with its own member in marital quarrels.

This hostility is often openly expressed at points in the marriage ceremony. The mock capture might indeed itself be interpreted in this way, except that it is an affair of young people and seems to be very light-hearted. In a Chinese wedding the bride is 'teased' by her new affines for some hours after she first enters her husband's home; in an Indian one it is the husband who has to put up with banter from his bride's female kin when he goes to fetch her. In the Chinese 'teasing' both partners are made to look absurd, but it is the bride who is the butt of personal comment and must remain composed and not complain. This performance is thought to

5. H. A. Junod, *The Life of a South African Tribe*, Vol. I., pp. 103–10.

have the ritual effect of ensuring domestic harmony for the future.

The Indians described by Oscar Lewis have a more tactful way of asserting the competing claims of the two sides to superiority by singing songs at the respective homes of the couple during the preparatory rites that they go through separately.

In African marriages straightforward instruction and admonition to the couple, or to one or other of them, may be mixed with insult or given in a form that conveys it. An example is what is significantly called 'the accusation' at a Nyoro wedding. This is a letter from the bride's father to the bridegroom's (not to the bridegroom himself, since the Nyoro are a people among whom no man has independent authority during his father's lifetime) which is read out by the girl's representative when she is brought to her husband's home. It may read as follows:

'Take the girl in accordance with the custom of our country. She is now yours and you may scold and beat her if necessary. Our daughter is yours. She is not strong yet, and she has not yet had a husband. She is ignorant of marriage, and her husband's father should advise and instruct her gently. If she quarrels with her husband, or if he is angry and finds fault with her, the dispute should be settled peacefully by her husband's father. She often suffers from an illness of the head and chest, and if this sometimes prevents her from working properly do not be angry with her. If she wishes to visit her relatives do not prevent her. If she turns out really badly do not beat her excessively; send her back to us and we will refund the bridewealth. She is not in the habit of visiting casually in other people's houses, nor does she attend beer parties, so if she acquires these bad habits the fault will be yours.'[6]

Henri Junod, the missionary, whose work in South Africa has become a classic, writes of 'a most strange duel' when a Tsonga bride arrived at her husband's homestead. 'Ha,' cry the groomsmen to the bride, 'as you are becoming the wife of

6. J. H. M. Beattie, 'Nyoro Marriage and Affinity', *Africa*, 1958, p. 9.

our brother and coming into our village, try and leave all your vices outside. Do not steal any longer.' 'Forsake your bad ways and become a good girl.' To this the bride's relatives shout in return: 'You have nothing to boast about. Stop wearying the people.' 'She is far too good for you.' 'Does not everyone know the wild pranks of your son and the dishonour of your family?'

Earlier, at the betrothal, there was a similar dialogue, beginning from the girl's side. 'Here we are; we bring you your dog. Here it is. With us she was reputed to be a good girl. Now we shall hear you every day say that she is lazy, does not know how to cook, has a host of lovers. . . . All right! Kill her! Kill your dog! Have you not bought it? She is a witch! Put her to the ordeal!' From the man's side: 'Yes, you are right. We shall beat her. But if her husband is too hard on her we shall try to deliver her. We shall do our best to protect her.' Then came an exchange of insults between the women on the two sides. Girl's side: 'You dogs, people of no consequence! You have not even a broken pot to remove the ashes from the fireplace. You can congratulate yourselves on getting such a good wife as this, a hard worker, a splendid cook, a nice and honest girl!' Boy's side: 'Yes, if you have exhorted her sufficiently perhaps she will give up her bad ways!' Girl's side: 'You talk of bad ways! Look at your son! What was he? A wild beast! We have come to cut off his tail and make a man of him.'

A final example comes from Gunther Wagner's account of marriage among some peoples of the Nyanza Province of Kenya, then called North Kavirondo. 'In place of the cordiality and mutual politeness which ordinarily prevail between hosts and guests', he writes, 'both parties in this case adopt an exceedingly contemptuous and haughty attitude towards one another.'[7] Here the bride's party take the initiative. On the way they sing songs which imply that they are afraid the bridegroom's people are too poor to provide them with proper entertainment. When they arrive they may criticize, still in song, both the hospitality and the homestead, as well

7. G. Wagner, *The Bantu of North Kavirondo*, Vol. I, 1949, p. 415.

as the bridegroom's appearance and the alleged inadequacy of the bridewealth paid. Some would regard this aspect of marriage ceremonies as a kind of safety-valve, an opportunity of expressing genuinely hostile sentiments in a context in which they are conventionally required to be taken in good part, as if the offensive words were known to be mere jokes. This is what Radcliffe-Brown called 'privileged disrespect', and he said it was commonly found in relationships where reasons for hostility were combined with an obligation of friendly behaviour.

The Unity of Affines

But there are also expressions of unity and symbols of the desire for it. All the exchanges of gifts and hospitality between the groups of kin who are to be linked in affinity both express friendly relations and contribute to create them. Of course there is room for ambivalence here too: is the return prestation good enough? But to make or receive a gift is a public affirmation of friendship, whatever private feelings may be concealed. Commensality – eating together – or eating the food that someone has cooked is the expression of unity par excellence. We associate this perhaps most with a caste system where castes mark themselves off by the refusal of commensality with outsiders, but that is the obverse of a much more widely recognized principle. Reconciliation feasts put an end to quarrels, or to the public prosecution of quarrels. An interesting rite of incorporation of the outsider is that in which a Bemba husband, who has up to that point been forbidden to eat food cooked by his mother-in-law, is formally presented with dishes of every kind of food, a ceremony which marks the removal of the prohibition.

Perhaps the clearest affirmation of separateness followed by union is the Indian procedure whereby the boy's and girl's families have their separate feasts before the bridegroom's procession is welcomed and feasted at the bride's home. The principle is beautifully illustrated in the case of the Kandyan Sinhalese, where, as was mentioned, close kin marry with little formality and unrelated families with much; a couple of cross-cousins may have grown up in the same house. A marriage of cross-cousins may be so informal as to be barely noticed, but if it is celebrated there will be – and can be – only one feast. When unrelated people marry they follow the same practice as in India, giving two separate feasts followed by a joint one.

M. N. Srinivas, who has analysed in detail the rituals of the Coorgs of Southern India, describes a sequence of rituals that has the same significance, being performed first separately, though in the identical way, for the two partners and then by the bridegroom for the bride. The *Murta* ritual, which used to be performed at every life crisis, is now done only at marriage. It consists of an offering of milk and rice, the presentation of a gold coin, and a formal salutation to the person to whom the ritual is addressed. The kinsmen of bride and groom perform this rite of solidarity towards their own member, and then the groom does it for the bride.

At Coorg weddings the fathers of the couple do not meet. Some time afterwards each is entertained to a feast by the other's family; this is called 'knowing the relatives'. The visiting to and fro and exchange of hospitalities more typical of Africa is not mere play-acting, despite the many prescribed actions that accompany it. It does make people better and better acquainted as the time between betrothal and marriage goes on. Evans-Pritchard, who first remarked that although the payment of bridewealth legalizes a marriage it is not merely or primarily the requirement to return it that keeps a marriage in being, writes of the Nuer: 'The new social ties of conjugality and affinity are made stronger by each payment and by each ceremony, so that a marriage which is insecure at the beginning of the negotiations becomes surer with every new payment and rite; both sides, by the giving and receiving of cattle, and by joint participation in the rites, becoming more deeply committed to bringing about the union.'[8]

Where work parties of young people go to the home of the

8. E. E. Evans-Pritchard, op. cit., p. 59.

future affines, as is done by the Logoli in Kenya, this must have the same effect, as well perhaps as that of formally demonstrating the recognition by both youth and girl of the nature of the contribution each must make to the joint household. The young men's work parties here are not to be regarded as marriage prestations which earn rights over the bride. During the betrothal period both the youth and the girl go with parties of their friends to work at the home of their future affines. The boys do such odd jobs as they are asked, the girls work in the fields. The future bridegroom is not expected to do much work himself, and Wagner says the purpose of this visit is to show his father-in-law that he has friends he can rely on; this would certainly be the purpose of bringing as many as he could. Ritual restrictions surround these visits; neither may eat at the other's home, and the girls come without their hoes, to demonstrate that they are making no claim to own the land they dig.

One might finally mention a rite which expresses the future unity of the affines with a direct reference to commensality. This was seen by Wagner, though only once, among the Vugusu of the Kenya–Uganda border. The bride's mother put meat and millet porridge in a basket and gave it to a younger woman of her lineage, who put it on her head (as African women do when they carry anything) and then passed it to the bride, who did the same and passed the basket to a sister of the bridegroom. It was passed back in the same order, then handed to the sister-in-law, who ate what she could of the contents and gave the rest to the bride's mother. One of the elders said this was 'to show that in future the bride and groom's kin will help one another with food and freely give things to one another without quarrelling.'[9]

Fathers sometimes take part in the weddings of their children and sometimes not. In the Coorg ceremony, as was mentioned, the crucial discussion of the rights and duties of the bride is conducted by men who do not belong to either family but have the recognized relationship of 'family

9. G. Wagner, *The Bantu of North Kavirondo*, Vol. I, 1949, p. 425.

friend'.[10] The Nyoro who goes with the bride to make the 'accusation' is not her father but one of his kinsmen.

Anthropologists have not offered reasons for this, and perhaps there is no need of reasons. But there is one remarkable case, among the Bedouin of Cyrenaica, which has been interpreted by Emrys Peters.[11] Here the father of a bridegroom, or of any man attending a marriage ceremony, pretends not to know what is going on. The tent in which the ceremony is performed is pitched at some distance from that of the bridegroom's father, allegedly so that 'he shall not see it', although it cannot possibly be concealed from view. And in various ways the new husband is expected to behave towards his father as if he was still an unmarried son. In the early morning he leaves his wife and returns to his father's tent, so that it is that tent he appears from when the camp awakes. He still eats with his father. All this is expressly said by the Bedouin to be a way of sparing the father's feelings by letting him pretend that nothing has changed, an attitude that they also adopt in the face of certain heinous offences. Peters's explanation is that when he marries, although he is still as closely subject to his father's authority as he was before, a man enters on the status which up till then has distinguished his father from him. He has his own tent in which he can offer protection and hospitality to others. He has a father-in-law who can help him and yet does not exercise parental authority. Even this slight diminution in his power is something that the father finds hard to endure. Moreover the marriage celebrations express the younger generation's defiance of the older, for example by the loud singing of lewd songs, which break the rule that young men must not refer to sexual matters in the presence of their elders.

10. See page 102.

11. E. Peters, 'Aspects of the Family among the Bedouin of Cyrenaica', in *Comparative Family Systems*, ed. M. F. Nimkoff, 1965.

The Union of the Couple

On the whole African ethnography does not tell us much about rites which symbolize the union of the couple. But they are mentioned by our two authorities on marriage ceremonies combined with puberty rites, Audrey Richards and Monica Wilson. Such a symbol mentioned by the latter is the ritual washing by the couple, their hands being held together, with medicated water; the medicine, a seed called *ikipiki*, itself symbolizes kinship. On other occasions a woman washes in this way with her father, mother or young brother to assert kinship. The meaning of this rite at marriage is, said a Nyakyusa, 'My wife has come. She is now my relative.'

Comparable with the Nyakyusa washing together is the Bemba inauguration of the 'marriage-pot'. Both are symbols of union, but otherwise their significance is very different. The Nyakyusa rite creates kinship; the Bemba one directly initiates the socially sanctioned sexual union by the first performance of a rite of purification that the couple must perform after intercourse for the rest of their married life.

Symbols directly referring to joining are common in Indian marriage rites. The couple's thumbs, or their clothes, may be tied together. In China and Japan they drink from two cups fastened together. Both in India and China an essential preliminary to marriage is the casting of the horoscopes of the couple – that is the calculation of the influences that were operative at the time of the birth of each, from which it is supposed their respective destinies can be predicted. A couple whose horoscopes are not compatible ought not to marry, but there are ways of getting over this difficulty. More than one astrologer can be consulted; they do not all give the same interpretation. In China it is even possible simply to lay the horoscopes side by side on the domestic altar and wait to see if anything untoward happens; if it doesn't the marriage goes ahead.

In some Indian weddings the bride holds the two horoscopes in her hand, and at the auspicious moment, a time determined by the astrologers, the Brahmin priest puts the bridegroom's hand over them amid the applause of the assembled company. This is the dramatic climax of the wedding, although, as was mentioned earlier, it is the walking seven times round the sacred fire that ritually seals it. In a Coorg wedding the bridegroom finds his bride in the kitchen, the women's domain, of her home, wearing tied to her sari a purse with gold coins which her mother has given her. He removes this and gives her another in its place. Then he leads her out of the kitchen, holding her right hand in his.

Since the end of marriage is conceived to be the socially approved procreation of children, it may seem surprising that nothing has been said so far about symbols of fertility. If Sir James Frazer had been writing this book they would have been his first concern. When people pray to ancestral or other spirits to bless the marriage they imply, if they do not state, that that is what they mean by blessing (as the Victorians also did). The Nuer, pre-empting the future in their Nilotic way by asserting what they want to see, announce to the ancestors that the bride *will* bear a male child.

The Nyakyusa puberty ritual, which Monica Wilson has described in such detail, has as its avowed purpose the fertility of the bride, though instruction in wifely behaviour is incidental to it. The first action in it is for the girl to take into her lips a strong-tasting root wrapped in a leaf with salt in it and pull it in with her teeth so that the salt trickles into her mouth. This is thought to be a protection against pain in intercourse and in menstruation and its symbolism is obvious. It is not 'unconscious'; this is the Nyakyusa explanation. Leaves of plantain and sweet banana, symbolic of male and female, are used at many points in the ritual. The girl kneels on them before finally leaving the seclusion hut and eats roast bananas sprinkled with the *ikipiki* seeds of kinship. The banana represents the penis and eating symbolizes intercourse. When she washes before leaving the seclusion hut the water is poured on a leaf on which *ikipiki* has been sprinkled in the form of a cross; the two arms of the cross are said to represent male and female. The jumping over fire was also said by some Nyakyusa to be an intercourse symbol as well as a test of virginity. But there is a sense in which every detail of the ritual bears on fertility, in that any omission may, it is believed, anger the high god or the spirits of the ancestors, who will show their anger by making the new wife barren.

Although more and more anthropologists are turning their attention to the symbolism of ritual, for some reason they have generally concentrated on anything rather than marriage. A striking exception is Monica Wilson's *Rituals of Kinship among the Nyakyusa* (1957), from which this last example is taken. We can expect the field studies of the future to probe deeper than the kinds of obvious symbolism that I have discussed here.

CHAPTER 8

THE OUTSIDER

WHERE people are organized in lineages, and even sometimes where they are not, one partner in a marriage must be
an outsider to the group among which he or she goes to live.
Where the woman is the outsider a large part of marriage
ritual is concerned, as the previous chapter showed, with
her passage from the home where she grew up as a daughter
to the one where she is to live as a wife; in some cases the
ritual emphasizes a complete transfer to a new allegiance,
but in many it expresses not only reluctance to break the ties
with her childhood home but her right to maintain them.
The Coorg handing over of the eleven pebbles is a charming
example.

Even after the marriage ceremony there may be formal
assertions of the wife's continuing link with her own family.
Sometimes the new household is not set up for a considerable
time. Something has been said already about the sharing of
food as an expression of unity. Its converse is the imposition
of prohibitions on eating food cooked by one's new affines.
One way of recognizing the full admission of the stranger is
the gradual lifting of such prohibitions. This mode of gradual incorporation is more common when the husband is the
outsider, but sometimes one can see the removal of food
taboos also as a stage in that of a wife.

My ending of the discussion of marriage ritual with the
ceremony of formal transfer of the bride will have seemed
arbitrary to readers who already know some of the ethnography that I have used. But it was done deliberately so as
to emphasize how slow the process of the admission of the
outsider, as well as that of her detachment (when a woman is
in question) from her own family may be. But there are very
great differences between different societies in the extent,
and the sharpness, of the separation of a wife from her kin.

Wives as Outsiders

The wife as outsider usually has to work her passage in the secular sense by earning the approval either of her mother-in-law or, if her husband is a polygynist, of a senior wife, and when she is a newcomer she may be required to observe strict and onerous rules of respect towards her affines. And, however much she may have been formally incorporated into her husband's group, she is always, or for a long time, the 'outsider' in more than one sense. Wives bear the brunt of the conflicts of interest that arise in the joint family system where married brothers live in the same household under the authority of their father. In such a household, which is the traditional ideal in India, the component families often resent the father's decisions in the allocation of income, and sometimes insist on the partition of the joint property. It is the brothers who demand this, but the ideal of agnatic solidarity is preserved by the pretence that what has made it necessary is quarrels between wives.

Maurice Freedman, writing of a similar type of joint family in China, says that this is not fiction but truth; brothers are fiercely competitive for their share of the common patrimony, but they conceal their hostility in deference to the Confucian family ideal and let their wives, as outsiders, do the fighting for them.[1] Nevertheless, they blame women for being quarrelsome, and of course their own husbands don't like quarrelling with them – and the marriage ritual includes symbols of tranquillity which Freedman sees as an expression of desperate anxiety for something that experience has shown to be unattainable. The Confucian ideal was expressed in traditional Japan by the principle that a wife who displeased her husband's parents could be got rid of even if there was no dissension between her and her husband; the contrast between obligations to insiders and those to outsiders could hardly be more clearly stressed. But there is a catch in the argument here. In practice the member of the household who objects to the young wife will be the husband's mother, not his father – in fact, an

1. M. Freedman, *Chinese Lineage and Society*, 1966, p. 46.

outsider herself. She is the outsider who has worked her passage and eventually become the household authority as far as any younger woman is concerned. A Chinese wife, after her husband dies, may become the manager of the estate owned jointly by him and his sons.

In an African patrilineal society the extended family homestead, where a man's sons and their wives live together, is not usually so closely controlled by the patriarch, and we do not read of quarrelling between wives as the excuse for their husbands to set up independent homes. But wives as outsiders are made to bear the brunt of family troubles in another way. If a member of the household is sick, and the sickness is ascribed to someone's resentment that has borne fruit in witchcraft, a woman – an outsider – is more readily suspected than one of the solidary group of agnatic kinsmen. Or so we have been told; but a possibly more simple explanation is that witchcraft is believed to be a recourse of people with grudges against their fellows, and in a polygynous household many women do have grudges.

Let us return to the process of the assimilation of the outsider and the gradual severance, more or less complete, of a wife from her own kin. (A husband, though he may be an outsider in the homestead, is never expected to be detached from his lineage.)

In the village near Delhi described by Oscar Lewis[2] a bride is taken back to her home more than once before she finally settles at her husband's. In this case a significant factor is the age of the couple; they are generally betrothed very young, married while still young, and do not set up house for some years more. Lewis gives fourteen as the average marriage age for a boy, thirteen for a girl. After the bride has been taken in procession to her husband's home and the couple have together worshipped at all the shrines in his village, her brother comes to visit them, and takes her home on the following day. For another two or three years, until her parents think she is old enough, she stays at home living just as she did before (this is enough to demonstrate that the

2. O. Lewis, op. cit., pp. 185ff.

lamentations at parting at the wedding are primarily symbolic, though some people are said to find them so affecting
that they try to avoid witnessing a girl's departure). Then
they let her husband fetch her, again for only a few days.
Again her brother comes for her, and this time when she gets
home she is greeted with songs denigrating her husband's
house and his kin. She has a year at home, then a few months
with her husband, and after she has finally gone to him she
goes home for visits at a number of festivals. But when she is
with her husband nobody from home may visit her except
her younger brother. A shorter sequence of visits to and fro
by the couple together, escorted this time in each case by an
older relative from the household to which they are going, is
described in Zekiye Eglar's study of a Punjabi village
north-west of Lahore.[3] But in both these examples women
visit their parents for every family celebration and for some
seasonal rituals as well.

In these Indian examples the sexual and domestic union
are established together. In Africa this is not always so. After
her marriage has been formally consummated, a rite which
is usually held some time after the marriage ceremony and
the sacrifice of the wedding ox, a Nuer girl returns to her
own home and must stay there until she has borne and
weaned a child. During this time she is at home and her
husband is the outsider. Her parents build her a hut where
they can sleep together, but he must not be seen by them, let
alone eat with them, so he stays at some other homestead in
her village, and waits there till after dark; and he must be
away before dawn. When he is not coming the girl sleeps
together with her unmarried sisters, and when she hears he is
coming she feigns to take no interest. Thus she and her
parents pretend that nothing has happened rather as the
Bedouin father does in Cyrenaica, if in a less unexpected
way; what they pretend is that the girl is not going to leave
them after all. The husband too is pretending to be still a gay
young bachelor and living the same life at home that he did
before. His wife can visit him openly on formal occasions; at

3. Z. Eglar, *A Punjabi Village in Pakistan*, 1960.

harvest time she brings him coverings for the grain that is spread out to dry, and when the first millet is ready she makes porridge and takes it to him. When her child is born she brings it to her husband and stays a few days in his homestead, though there is no separate hut there for her yet; this is built only when she weans the child and leaves her parents. But if they want it she must leave the child behind, to stay with them until it is grown up.

Evans-Pritchard interprets this long-drawn-out process as a gradual coming together of the kin on both sides with their new affine, and this is one aspect of it, as it is of the Indian procedure, but I would add to this the element of reluctance to part with the daughter, since this is so often expressly emphasized. Indeed it could be argued that the payment of bridewealth might be regarded rather as a 'consolation' than, as it has so often been considered, a 'compensation'.

The prolonged stay of a Nuer bride at home is unusual, but it is not unique. Curiously enough – but this is something that often happens in the field of ethnography – the other instances on record concern peoples who live nowhere near the Nuer and are not particularly like them in mode of life and organization. They are found in northern Nigeria and in Mali. Of the Dogon in the latter country Denise Paulme has written that a woman was traditionally expected to live with her own parents until she had borne three children, and that during that time the couple were never together for more than *de courts instants*. This certainly sounds difficult, especially when one remembers that it is the rule in most of rural Africa that a couple should not resume intercourse while the wife is suckling a child, and that suckling commonly lasts three years. The first child was left with its grandparents, and should stay there until the death of the grandparent of the same sex.

In contrast with these examples there are societies in which it is essential at this juncture – the bearing of a child – for the outsider to be brought right inside. To the Tallensi, although a child is made jurally a member of its father's lineage by the payment of bridewealth, it must be made ritu-

ally so by being born under the protection of the lineage
ancestors, and reared there in the early months that are so
dangerous in countries where many infants die. It is a rule
that it must not be born at the home of its mother's lineage.
The two descent groups, as Fortes sees it, 'represent opposed
forces in its social world', and matrilateral kinship ties –
which, as he shows us, are strong – 'must not be allowed to
become a threat to lineage ties'. But this does not mean that,
for other purposes, a married woman is severed from her own
parents. They may send for her if there is serious sickness at
her own home, and they must send for her if someone there
dies; then she must go even if she has to leave a baby behind.

Occasionally a wife may be more completely severed from
her own home. One aspect of this severance may be the idea
that for her to die there would bring disaster on its inhabi-
tants. This is the belief of the Gusii in Kenya; they have a
proverb, 'A woman should not grow grey hairs in her father's
home', but in addition they are so afraid of the untoward
consequences of her dying there that they do not like to have
their married kinswomen come to stay. To make effective
this severance from the old home and committal to the new
they used to perform an additional ritual called *enyangi*
after which it was impossible to dissolve a marriage. Philip
Mayer[4] saw this in 1947 and said it was the most elaborate
of all Gusii rites. A couple need not make *enyangi* until they
have been married for years; they might never do it. Not to
have done it did not affect their status in everyday life, but
those who had not were debarred from performing certain
ritual functions, and in that sense could be said to be not
fully adult. Before *enyangi* could be held for a couple all the
bridewealth due had to be paid; hence there could be no
question of any demand on that score for the return of the
bride. At *enyangi* iron ankle-rings were tied on the wife's
legs, which she would wear for the rest of her life. They
proclaimed her as a fully and finally married woman. If she
broke her marriage she would have to take them off, and this

4. 'Privileged Obstruction of Marriage Rites among the Gusii', *Africa*,
1950, pp. 113–25.

T–E

was an action liable to supernatural punishment. Also she was given a new name. Her husband could now no longer annul the marriage by demanding the bridewealth back.

These rites were marked by expressions of hostility of the kind that have already been noted in wedding ceremonies. And since the parties to *enyangi* already knew one another and had had time to develop dislike as well as liking, the shafts were barbed and the abuse was more than joke. As in many ceremonies a man – the 'marriage priest' – presided over the rites, and the senior men of both lineages were present. Yet there is a sense in which this was essentially a women's rite. Women on both sides – notably the wife and her mother-in-law – were allowed to hold up the proceedings as they pleased, sometimes demanding gifts and sometimes gratuitously. On one day at *enyangi* the husband had to come in procession with his friends to the wife's home; on the next she went back to his. At her home the husband would be met outside the house by his wife and her friends, shrieking obscenities and taunting him with sexual inadequacy; no one could stop them, they went on as long as they liked. At his, the mother-in-law and other married women (members of the husband's homestead and village, not his lineage) would keep the wife out and upbraid her for laziness and disrespect to elders. This was recognized as a contest. 'Let her trouble us tonight,' said an elder of a bridegroom's family to Mayer. 'When she comes to our place we will see to it.'

But an essential element in *enyangi* was that the wife must 'show her love' for her husband by performing a rite, in itself not very spectacular. She handed him a calabash, and he gave her in return a piece of millet porridge (millet porridge is solid); and the following morning she drank with him from a loving-cup. In view of the general tenor of *enyangi* this might perhaps seem more like a vow than a declaration of affection. But it was in the latter light that the Gusii saw it, and at this part of the ceremony, which the wife could again obstruct and delay, the bridegroom's friends would be really concerned whether she loved him.

Enyangi then was the final privileged occasion for the expression of a hostility of which the Gusii are well aware; they are among the people who say 'those whom we marry are those whom we fight'. Between the people who were to be committed to living together – wife and husband, daughter and mother-in-law – this was, as the Gusii themselves saw it, a final expression of resentments which would (should?) be silenced from then on. Presumably, if a wife considered her grievances too great to be borne, she would not allow the ceremony to be made for her at all.

There was more licence for express provocation in *enyangi* than in the wedding ceremonies described earlier, but the ceremony itself had restraints built into it. In the first place, the exchange of insults was confined to women, and the bridegroom himself was the only man to be directly insulted. Then it was considered absolutely essential that no blood be shed; if it were, the whole costly ceremony would have to be done again. The elders who came to witness the 'showing of love' and the tying of the ankle-rings sat in two lines facing one another with two sacred beer pots between them, and the husband's party brought with them a man called the 'watcher' whose duty it was to stop arguments before they went too far. Mayer's final comment is one that could be applied to many of the wedding ceremonies described in the preceding chapter. The marked symmetry of rites and entertainments suggests the effort that is being made to cement friendship. The order of *enyangi* prescribes that feasts and sacrifices are held alternately at the two homesteads; that portions of sacrificial and other meat are exchanged; small formal processions are constantly coming and going, and objects of religious significance carried to and fro.

But the ritual finished with an injunction to the couple not to look back as they walked away to the husband's home. Her kin could visit her there, but she had now become an 'insider' to a greater degree than most African wives. She could not be buried at her father's home without bringing disaster upon it, and to avoid this risk she must not spend her

last days anywhere within the territory of her father's clan.
Gusii believe that for an affine to be buried in one's homestead brings disaster; his line would increase at the expense
of the homestead owner. How more clearly could it be recognized that the wife has become an insider? Another way in
which this is shown is that if a woman is killed it is her
husband and not her father who is entitled to compensation.
If a sacrifice has to be made to a spirit supposed to have
afflicted a woman with sickness, it must be made by a
brother of her husband, not of her own – unless the sickness
is interpreted as a punishment for something she did before
she was married; in that case, her own brother must make
the necessary sacrifice. Women married by *enyangi* shave
their heads at the funerals of men of their husband's lineage,
but not in their own.[5]

Ceremony or no, a new bride has to work her passage in
almost any pre-industrial society. Always this entails taking
more than her share of arduous tasks; often exaggeratedly
formal expressions of respect are expected of her. It is striking that a new bride should be so often described as a servant
for her mother-in-law (herself, as was noted, a one-time outsider), as if to secure one had been the principal aim of the
marriage.

The extreme of formal respect behaviour is illustrated from
some Bantu peoples of South Africa. Monica Wilson has described the rules for a Pondo bride. They go far beyond what
anthropologists more commonly mean by 'avoidance' – rules
that in effect prevent the parties to a difficult relationship
from meeting in direct confrontation. The Pondo girl must
'respect' in this sense not only her husband's senior relatives
but everything in the homestead that is associated with
them. She must not utter their names, nor words that sound
like them, she must not set foot on the right side (the men's
side) of a hut belonging to any of them. This may even
conflict with the work required of her, if she has to leave half
a hut unswept. She cannot chase after dogs or pigs doing
damage in the forbidden area, only throw things at them.

5. P. Mayer, *The Lineage Principle in Gusii Society*, 1949, pp. 7–8.

She has to make great detours through long grass, getting her skirts soaked in the dew, so as not to walk by the right side of a hut.

As for the bride's daily duties, she is expected to be the first up in the morning and fetch water for the household, then put in time sweeping until the other women wake up and she goes to the fields with them. She must go every day for firewood, and when wild vegetables to eat with the porridge are scarce in winter she must go the long walk to find them. She does more than her share of grinding and cooking and helps in repairing the huts. An old man nicknamed his son's wife 'the bell', because 'now my wife just sits still and calls when she wants anything, just like a white lady ringing the bell'.[6]

The only consolation for the daughter-in-law is that one day she can hope to be a mother-in-law, and in the nature of things this will not be for a long time. This is equally true – perhaps even more widely true – in India, China and Japan. In Japan there is a way out for some girls; only the eldest son is expected to live in his father's house, and kind parents will try to marry their daughters to younger sons. In these days the problem arises only in the rural areas; in Japan's great cities young couples live on their own. Several writers have remarked that the harshness of mothers-in-law is a way of getting their own back for the sufferings of their youth.

Husbands as Outsiders

Men are less amenable than women to the idea that they are outsiders in the place where they are expected to live, and this is responsible for some of the complications and instabilities that are found in matrilineal societies. The matrilineal societies in Africa show a remarkable variety of rules about the place where a married couple ought to live, and at any rate one interesting example of the gradual admission of the outsider into the status of a full member of the homestead.

6. M. Wilson, *Reaction to Conquest*, 1936, pp. 33ff.

The most striking way of dealing with the situation is that of the Ashanti in Ghana, where husband and wife may live in separate houses for many years or all their lives. But, as Fortes has pointed out, the principles that have to be balanced are the same there as in any other matrilineal society. Malinowski wrote of the conflict between mother-right and father-love. Fortes, preferring to express himself in terms of social structure, refers to 'the balance struck between the obligations of marriage and parenthood on the one hand, and those due to matrilineal kin on the other',[7] but he too remarks that a man commonly loves his own children more than the sisters' sons who are legally dependent on him. But the group consisting of his wife, her (their) children and her brothers is constantly seeking to assert its autonomy and protect its interests; and he and his sisters and their children are doing the same. Especially in more conservative places brothers and sisters may live all their lives together in one house.

So the children of one mother keep together as long as they can, and when a couple are first married the girl still lives at home. But this is not because, as with so many patrilineal societies, she puts off assuming her wifely duties. She works on her husband's farm and cooks his food, and sends it to him by a child messenger, a little brother or sister. If she is still living at her home when her own children are old enough, they will live with her and will carry to their father, and eat with him, the food she has cooked for them all. Unlike some matrilineal husbands he would think it shameful to live in her home. It is when their children are growing up that wives most often leave their own homes for their husbands', but an adult man is expected as soon as he can to build a house where his mother will live with him and look to him as her main support.

But in most matrilineal societies, as in patrilineal ones, people think that husband and wife should live in the same house. The question then is where this should be. There is a rule that people must not marry within their own lineage,

7. M. Fortes, 'Time and Social Structure', in *Social Structure*, ed. M. Fortes, 1949, p. 70.

and there is an ideal that lineage members should keep together; so that one or other partner must leave the lineage home. In patrilineal societies it is the woman who lives the rest of her life as the outsider on her husband's ground. The man is an outsider, of course, when he visits her family, and this is recognized in a number of rules of formal behaviour. In matrilineal societies he is the permanent outsider, the parent from whom his children do not take their lineage membership. This is an argument for requiring him to be the one who leaves his own ground and moves to his wife's, and often it is the rule that married life should at least begin at the wife's home. Many African languages have a word that is loosely translated 'owner', and in the village of the 'matrilineal belt' they distinguish between 'owners' – lineage members – and others; in the Yao and Cewa languages the 'others' are 'husbands of owners'. I shall never forget walking into a Cewa homestead and asking the first man I met whose home it was. 'I can't tell you,' he said, 'I'm only a husband.' Of course he didn't mean that he didn't know; but it would not have been appropriate for the outsider to go giving information to a stranger.

The position of the husband as outsider is more complicated than that of the wife. A woman may hope to end her days as the domineering matriarch (in the popular sense of the word) of a large homestead, but her authority remains domestic. A man *expects* to exercise domestic authority, but he may also be *required* to exercise authority in wider spheres, over the junior members of his lineage and their spouses. In a patrilineal society they are grouped around him; in a matrilineal society, is he to live at his sisters' home or his wife's?

The problem has been described as a conflict between *familial* and *lineal* principles. Attempts to solve it show remarkable variety, even among peoples who are near neighbours, as are those of Zambia and Malawi. One way is the paradoxical one in which the husband first comes to his wife's home as an outsider and later, when he has earned recognition as an insider, is allowed to take his wife away with him.

This is the traditional rule among the Bemba of Zambia and the Yao and Cewa of Malawi. But it works out rather differently for Bemba on the one hand and Yao or Cewa on the other. As long ago as 1931, when Audrey Richards was working among the Bemba, their customary marriage arrangements were being disregarded by young men who spent much of their time away from home working on the Copper Belt, and it is quite possible that nobody now follows the old rule. This was that the future husband came to live at his bride's home some years before they were married, and worked at her father's orders as he continued to do after they were married. The girl went on gardening and cooking with her mother for some time after she had set up house with him. For the first year or so after the couple were living together they were merged in working teams controlled by the girl's parents – sons-in-law cutting down branches to make gardens and building granaries, wives with their sisters hoeing and cooking. At the end of that time the husband could have his own garden and the wife her own cooking fire, ritually lighted for her by her mother. But it might be years before the performance of the final rite removing all barriers, a beer feast at which the husband danced opposite his mother-in-law. Before this he must have begotten two children, but that might have happened long before. 'You have entered our family,' he would be told. 'You have built yourself a house.' But it was then – because this ceremony signified complete approval of him as a satisfactory husband with whom their daughter could be secure of good treatment – that he became entitled, if he wished, to take her away to his own lineage home.

A Cewa or Yao village, as was just mentioned, is ideally the home of a small lineage which 'owns' it. Its headman should be the senior man of the lineage. He is expected to 'cherish his people', to smooth over quarrels, matrimonial and other, and so keep the village at peace. As a lineage senior he has especial responsibility for the women of his lineage and their children. He must appear in court if one of them is involved in a court case. One of his most important duties is to take the appropriate steps if any of them falls sick; he should consult a diviner as to the cause and make the sacrifice recommended. This description implies that a lineage senior is always the headman of a village. But how can he be if he has to live in his wife's village? The answer, of course, lies in the rule that he can take his wife away with him if her lineage senior agrees. But sometimes he does not agree, and sometimes the husband will then leave and let the marriage break up. This seems to be becoming more common; it is certain that husbands expect to take their wives home earlier than they used, and it is in the early years of a marriage that it is most likely to break up. Another possibility is less common: a lineage senior may go on living with his wife but visit his own village when there is trouble there. The answer that solves all problems is to marry a cross-cousin, a woman whose father is a lineage member and lives in the lineage village; then one can meet both the requirements of matriliny at the same time. And things are not too difficult if the wife's home is close at hand.

Yet another solution is to say, matriliny or no, wives go with their husbands so that brothers can live all their lives together. This is the rule among the Ndembu in Zambia, of whom it has been written that 'each village represents an attempt to establish a patriarchal settlement in the teeth of basic matrilineal descent'.[8] Here the status of outsider descends to the next generation; it is the children who are outsiders in their father's village, and will very likely go home with their mother when he dies or even as soon as they are adult (as Cewa brought up in their fathers' villages also do). The Tonga in northern Malawi call a married woman 'just a daughter-in-law', and she is as much or as little separated from her own home as she would be in a patrilineal society; the difference is that she would be more likely to go home if her husband died, and that her children would probably go with her, as they would not be likely to do where all their inheritance rights were at their father's place. Indeed they might be fetched home by their lineage seniors. The

8. V. W. Turner, *Schism and Continuity in an African Society*, 1957, p. 238.

crucial disability of a Ndembu or Cewa living in his father's village is that he can never become headman there.

The effect of such an arrangement, among both these peoples, is to create competition between maternal and paternal kin to have the children of any given marriage live among them. It is the headmen of villages who seek to attract followers; not only by having their own sisters and sisters' children return to them, as they are entitled to expect, but by persuading their own sons to stay. A man may be dependent on his father even though he is not a member of his lineage; his father as well as his mother's brother can give him a share of lineage land and so keep him at home; and in a Tonga (Malawi) village, although he is not an 'owner', he is not likely to be turned out even after his father dies. A headman who is getting old can delegate his authority to his son; again the son cannot inherit his position, but he may enjoy a considerable period of power and influence.

Men in a matrilineal society, then, to a large extent get around the disadvantages that the status of outsider might seem at first sight to entail. In patrilineal ones, though a man is never expected to live under the authority of his father-in-law, the 'outsider' status of a son-in-law is formally emphasized on any occasion when he meets his wife's family. Beattie[9] in writing of Nyoro marriage procedure has remarked that the suitor, as an individual, has to confront as a group the men in whose lineage he is seeking a bride. They are, on this formal, public occasion, a solidary band of agnatic kin. They are giving a daughter to *him*, not to him-and-his-agnates; they will give other daughters to men of other lineages. Sons-in-law cannot form a group; they are a bunch of outsiders all coming from different directions – and, of course, except on such solemn occasions as funerals, all the sons-in-law are not likely to be together at the home of their affines.

During the betrothal and marriage formalities, as was noted earlier, the Nyoro husband has to adopt a very humble attitude towards his affines and put up with displays of

9. J. Beattie, *Nyoro Kinship, Marriage and Affinity*, 1958.

superiority from them. As a son-in-law his position is somewhat less disagreeable. He must show formal respect to his parents-in-law, but so must they to him. But he is regarded as a 'child' not only by the couple whose daughter he has married, but by all members of the father's lineage, including those who are younger than he is, so that more deference must always come from his side. He must visit his father-in-law regularly, dressed in his best and bringing presents with him, and while at this man's home he must observe a grave demeanour, not whistle or shout, not refer to any sexual matter and not contradict him. Whereas demands on a Gisu husband are made only as long as he has not paid the full bridewealth, a Nyoro father-in-law can go on making them for ever; proverbs compare him with the Nyoro equivalent of the bottomless pit. Towards his wife's mother he must practise what anthropologists technically call 'avoidance': not see her or speak to her except through a third person. This custom, common to most African patrilineal societies, is one of the few that most laymen have heard of, and for some reason they find it supremely ridiculous. Actually it is a way of showing respect, more exaggerated than what is required in behaviour towards the wife's father because a respect relationship towards a person of opposite sex is normally more marked. It is a much more dignified way of dealing with a difficult relationship than going to a music-hall to laugh at mother-in-law jokes.

Though the marks of deference demanded by Nyoro custom may be extreme, the rule that a man must behave with unusual circumspection where he is an outsider in the home of his affines is general. It is the standard way of maintaining overtly friendly relations between people who may often have occasion for disagreement – for example over bridewealth debts or complaints by the wife against her husband. It parallels European customs, in formal situations where disagreement has to be expressed, of referring to people by office and not by name, addressing one another through the chairman, avoiding 'unparliamentary language', and the like.

No Outsiders?

It will be clear by now that marriage in societies divided into lineages has many implications – fascinating or tedious according to one's taste – that do not exist where descent is cognatic, as it is in western Europe and also in a large part of south-east Asia. For this or other reasons, anthropologists have given much less attention to the details of marriage and affinal relationships in cognatic societies. In some such societies, not only in the industrialized world, a couple, when they marry, go off and live where they please, so that there is no question of an outsider. But in others they do expect to live near people with whom they have some kind of kinship, and where there is no rule of unilineal descent that determines which partner is the outsider, we have to ask what is done in practice.

One answer comes from the Iban of Borneo, who only twenty years ago were living in most respects in accordance with their traditional customs. Like all the peoples of Borneo, the Iban live in 'long-houses'. A long-house is in fact like a terraced street of one-room houses with a common open space in front. It is raised on piles and approached by a ladder, which can be removed for defence. Each room in a long-house is the dwelling of a separate family and belongs to it alone. It is only architecturally that the whole can be described as *a* house; socially, as Derek Freeman, who has described Iban family organization, points out, it is more like a village.[10]

The Iban are monogamous, and so the domestic family is small. They have only one rule about where people are to live: whatever else happens, one of a couple's children *must* stay in the natal home and be joined there by a spouse (there are no unmarried children tending aged parents). Usually only one does. There is no rule as to who this should be, and in the long-houses where Freeman took census data the numbers of sons and daughters staying in the parental home were almost exactly equal.

10. J. D. Freeman, 'The Family System of the Iban of Borneo', in *The Developmental Cycle of Domestic Groups*, ed. J. R. Goody, 1958.

In this society the departure of a member of the family is an occasion, according to Freeman, of genuine, not ritualized, sorrow. An Iban speaking to him called it the casting away of one's father and mother. But the welcome of the outsider to the new family is early and complete. The first meal that the couple eat there is taken from a special dish, a family heirloom, that is used only on ritual occasions, and after the meal the plate is turned upside down in a ritual gesture that symbolizes the anchoring of the newcomer to the house. The person who marries out receives his share of inheritance in movable property and thenceforth has no more claims in the natal house; land to plant rice goes with the house in which one is living. It is for a man's own parents, not those of his wife, to decide when they shall make this gift and what they will give him; as far as his affines are concerned he has no need to work his passage to be accepted as an insider, and he may in time become the head of the household he has joined.

Another place where either husband or wife may be the outsider is Ceylon, where marriage is called by a different name according to which of the two it is: *binna* if the man lives in his wife's village and from her land, *diga* if she depends on him and comes to his home. Not many married couples actually live with the parents of either, though brothers-in-law may live together. As might be expected from general male attitudes, *binna* marriage is considered inferior, and only poor men make such marriages; yet they are very common.

Parents who control their daughters' marriages decide whether they shall marry *binna* or *diga*, so that this is a matter of strategy of the kind discussed in Chapter 5. What is the use of a son-in-law around the house? In effect he is a hired help who need not be paid. People look for a *binna* son-in-law if they have no sons of their own to work their land and no spare cash to pay labour. They allot to a son-in-law land that would not otherwise be worked. Eventually his wife will inherit this land, and so control what cash income it may produce; and their children will look to her and not to him for their inheritance. Obviously only a man who has not enough land to support a family will marry on those terms; he is not the equal of his wife's parents, as in Ceylon a *diga* married man is, but their inferior. Yet, in a sense, just because of this he is not an outsider. His inferiority is that of a junior member of the family; his status has been compared with that of an adopted son.[11]

In a conventional textbook much of the information given in this chapter would be found under some such heading as 'Rules of Residence'. Anthropologists who love polysyllables have invented a string of words to describe where a married couple are expected to, or do, live in relation to their senior kin. I offer this chapter as a demonstration that they can be dispensed with, but since those who read this book may go on to other books on the same subject I give a brief glossary. *Patrilocal* means living with somebody's father, but is used of patrilineal societies and *not* of Bemba husbands living with their fathers-in-law. *Matrilocal* means living with somebody's mother; in fact, with the wife's mother. But actually the important question is to what senior male kinsman a young couple are supposed to attach themselves; so we get *avunculocal*, meaning with somebody's uncle. But whose? Husband's or wife's? As has been shown, matrilineal societies may expect one or other. Some offered *uxori-avunculocal* to make it clear that it is the wife's mother's brother who is referred to. But despair then begot commonsense, and anthropologists agreed that what matters is simply whether the wife is expected to go to her husband's place, whatever that may be, or *vice versa*; from this we get *virilocal* and *uxorilocal*. Freeman offered *utrolocal* for a system where either was permitted, but this never caught on. But we have *duolocal* for arrangements such as those of the Ashanti where the couple have separate homes. *Neolocal* (in a new place) means they can live wherever they like.

11. N. Yalman, *Under the Bo Tree*, 1967, pp. 122–4.

CHAPTER 9

PLURAL MARRIAGES

Up to this point, for the sake of clarity, marriage has been discussed as a union of one man with one woman, and so it is generally defined. But there are societies in which it is possible for either a man or a woman to contract such a union with more than one partner at a time. Such a system is called *polygamy*, and the word refers to marriage and not to sexual relations. Thus, to speak of unfaithful spouses, whether men or women, as polygamous is inaccurate and can be very misleading. Sexual infidelity is regarded more or less severely in different societies, and usually, though not always, more severely in women than in men. Feminists resent this 'double standard'. But to say, as I heard it recently said, that the remedy would be to make both sexes *polygamous* is nonsense if the word is used in its correct sense.

There are two types of polygamy: *polygyny*, in which a man may have more than one wife, and *polyandry*, in which a woman may have more than one husband. The first is by far the most common, and has been referred to in passing at various points in this book. Also there are instances in which a man is permitted to add to his household women who are not in the full sense his wives, and others in which a woman is permitted to have sex relations with specified men other than her husband. These marginal cases will be discussed later in this chapter. I do not count them as marriage, as will be clear from what I have just said. If I am asked why, I fall back on the definition of marriage as a union which confers status and/or inheritance rights on the children who issue from it. All anthropologists will agree with me that mere tolerated sexual access to a married woman does not make a polygynous marriage.

Plural Husbands

The classical case of polyandry in a patrilineal society is that of Tibet. Here the rule is that brothers can be jointly married to a single wife. The wedding takes place when the eldest brother has reached the appropriate age; all the others ought to be present, but some are sometimes considered too young to be trusted to behave properly at a formal ceremony. Nevertheless the ritual confers on them too the status of husband. All husbands live in one house with the wife. Sometimes one of the younger brothers prefers to seek a wife elsewhere, and does so by becoming the husband of a woman who is the heiress to property (mainly land) because she has no brothers. Such a woman can choose her husbands, and in the nature of things they will not be a set of brothers. Her sons will inherit the property that came to her from her father. Another possibility for a younger son is to become a monk and so commit himself to a life of celibacy. All the husbands of a polyandrous wife are accounted equally the fathers of all her children, but on formal occasions when it is necessary for one man to perform the role of father it is the eldest who does so.

The advantage ascribed to polyandry of this type by the people who practise it is that it makes unnecessary the division of property between the families of a set of brothers. This is the same reason that has been given for the marriage of near kin – brother–sister marriage where this has been recorded and Arab marriage within the lineage. A further advantage sometimes mentioned is that a polyandrous husband who has to be away from home for trade or business has someone to leave in charge of his wife.

A very different type of polyandry is found among some of the non-Islamic peoples of northern Nigeria. This was first discovered by C. K. Meek, who held the post of Government Anthropologist there between the two world wars, in what is now called the Middle Belt – the part of the former Northern Region of Nigeria that was never wholly brought under control by the Fulani Emirs. Two of these peoples, the

Kadara and Kagoro, were studied more closely in 1950 by M. G. Smith.[1] Here husbands and wife do not live together in one household, nor are the men simultaneously married to the woman as brothers are in Tibet. The wife makes a second formal marriage and leaves her first husband's home. But this is not a case of divorce followed by a new marriage; in various ways it is clear that the first is held to be still in being. Superior authority, both British and Fulani, has sought to suppress the custom, and when Smith was there it was not being practised in its traditional form by the younger generation; however, it had been part of the experience of the older men and women and was by no means obsolete.

Kadara girls were betrothed as infants. Marriage prestations there were of two kinds. Before the marriage, while the bride was growing up, the husband had to give a fixed number of days each year in farm labour, and after it he had to present large pots of beer when a child was born and/or every three years. (I put it like this because the space between births in Africa, in the days when a couple did not resume intercourse till the child was weaned, was often reckoned as three years.)

The wife chose her next husband; that is to say a man sought her consent and then formally approached her father. If the latter agreed she ran away to her lover's village, and stayed with some kinsman of her father who lived there until a marriage feast was held, after which the first husband was informed. The second husband became liable for the gifts of beer to the father-in-law. The first ceased to make them, but he did not cease to call the woman his wife (nor she to call him her husband). The woman could go back and visit her first husband, and while she was there she behaved in every way as a wife. Thus, not only was the second marriage publicly and formally made, but the first was not dissolved. A woman was widowed by the death of either husband and should be inherited by his heir in either case.

1. M. G. Smith, 'Secondary Marriage in Northern Nigeria', *Africa*, 1953, pp. 298–323.

A woman's first husband was found within the local community of people who combine for the performance of important rituals. She could not take a second husband from within the community; her lover had to come from outside. Thus first husbands and wife-stealers, as they are sometimes called, belonged to distinct categories which could not overlap.

The Kagoro institution differs in some respects from the Kadara. They too betrothed their daughters in infancy, but here it was the guardian of the woman, her father or mother's brother, who arranged a second betrothal, this time with her consent, after she was married. The same public procedure was followed as in a first marriage, so that there was here no question of concealment from the husband. The wife and her new betrothed called each other by a name meaning 'the one who waits', and the two men called each other by a name meaning 'thing of trouble'. The second one had to make payments of various kinds, and the woman could not join him until these were completed. But he was allowed to visit her by stealth, and if the first husband caught him he was expected to treat him with the politeness due to a guest. When the payments were finished she was formally conducted to her new home by the kinsmen who arranged her betrothal. It seems that this marriage too might be made without the woman's consent, since Smith says the second husband could coerce her by kidnapping a child after one of his visits. By agreement with her second husband she could go back to the first for long spells, from six months to a year.

Here too the second husband must be found outside the local community which provides the first. As Smith points out, the effect of these rules concerns a wider field than that of marriage. In each case they divide the whole tribe into descent groups between which different kinds of relationship are prescribed, and thus provide the framework for the whole social structure.

For polyandry in a matrilineal system the Indian subcontinent provides the classic case in the Nayars of Malabar as they were in the eighteenth century, when we begin to have descriptions of them which go into some detail. The Nayar household of those days consisted exclusively of a matrilineal descent group, without any resident 'outsider' such as one finds in central Africa, and even without living-out husbands such as one finds in Ashanti. This has led some people to maintain that the Nayars, in that respect unique among the peoples we know, did not possess the institution of marriage.

The smallest Nayar descent groups held property in common and lived in one house under the authority of the oldest male member. Such a group consisted of brothers and sisters with the children and daughter's children of the sisters. But the brothers were away from home a good deal of the time, because they were professional soldiers employed in the wars of the small kingdoms to which they belonged. This must have been one reason why the question where husbands should live seems to have presented no problem.

All Nayar girls before puberty went through a ritual which in a certain sense was a marriage ceremony. The essence of this rite was that the crucial action of a marriage ritual in this part of India – the tying of a gold ornament (the *tali*) around the bride's neck – was performed for the girl by a man who would never be in the everyday sense her husband. She was secluded along with him for three days, and they might have sex relations if she was approaching puberty. After this the man need have no further contact with her, but when he died she and all her children had to observe the ritual of purification from the pollution of death, a ritual otherwise observed only for matrilineal kin.

Who were the fathers of her children then? A girl who had been through the *tali* rite was entitled to receive at her home as many lovers as she liked, provided they were of appropriate caste and not within the prohibited degrees of kinship. The ritual husband might, but need not be, one of them. The one strict rule was that she must not have a lover of lower caste. Nayar men, subject to the same prohibitions, could visit as many women as they chose (but this has not usually been taken to mean that Nayar society is poly-gynous).

A man would make gifts to the woman he visited, and was expected to make these publicly at festivals. But he had no responsibility for her maintenance, which was provided by her brothers; and he was not expected to continue the gifts when the relationship had ceased. When a woman had a child one or more of her lovers – those who thought they might be responsible for its paternity – would pay the fee of the midwife who delivered it. But all children were brought up wholly by their matrilineal kin. They called all their mother's current lovers/husbands by a word meaning 'lord'; the fact that they gave this mark of respect suggests that the status of these men can be equated with that of a hus-band/father. Another argument in this sense advanced by Kathleen Gough, who worked among the Nayar in 1947–9 and has made the most recent examination of the literature referring to them, is that the payment of the midwife's fee is a public acknowledgement of paternity; and since unions which contravene the rules of lineage exogamy and caste endogamy are strictly forbidden, it is clear that the caste status of children has to be secured by the recognition that their father was a man of appropriate caste and status. As I remarked in the first chapter, the determination of the status of a woman's children is one of the most important functions of a husband.

As Nigeria supplies a pendant to the patrilineal polyandry of the Tibetans, the Congo supplies one to the matrilineal polyandry of the Nayars. This is the case of the Lele of the Kasai basin, who have been described by Mary Douglas.

The Lele are among the societies in which girls are be-trothed in infancy to men of twenty or so, who then have to wait for their brides to grow up. The Lele maintain that this is not the only reason why young men have to wait for wives; they assert that their elders bestow the marriageable girls on one another. In any case they resent the long years they have to spend as bachelors, and plume themselves on their success in the seduction of married women. An institution which gives them a legitimate alternative is their polyandrous right to a 'wife of the village'.

A Lele village was divided into age-sets consisting of men born within a period of fifteen years or so. A new set was formed when a sufficient number of the younger generation were about eighteen (exact records of age were not kept). These young men would ask to be allotted a common wife, for whom they made a joint marriage payment of raffia cloths and built a hut for her to live in. The granddaughter of a village wife could be so allotted. Otherwise they found their own wife, abducting her from a neighbouring village. This, and the practice of polyandry itself, were frowned on by the authorities, and were made punishable by imprisonment just before Mary Douglas visited the Lele. Nevertheless she was able to obtain more complete information about the institution than anyone had before. It has parallels among neighbouring peoples.

Missionaries have written of the 'village wife' as *'une malheureuse'* condemned to prostitution. Mary Douglas found that her status, and also that of her children, was an honourable one carrying privileges with it; but she might be assigned to it while she was very young. It was preferable to obtain a village wife by capture, since this raised the prestige of the captor's village in relation to the one which lost a girl. When she was brought to the village she spent some time doing none of the ordinary domestic tasks, but sitting gossiping with the young men as they worked at weaving the raffia cloths in which marriage payments are made. She slept in turn with each member of the age-set, strictly in order of age. The number would depend upon the number in the set, from six to twelve – up to twenty in a big village. Meantime they, in a body, would be giving the appropriate services to her parents, and when she, at the time of her own choice, asked to set up house they jointly made the marriage payments.

The girl now chose from the whole set five or six men who would actually live in her house, and for whom she would cook, hoe and fetch water like an ordinary wife. Away from home she was still the wife of the village, and any man could have intercourse with her without infringeing anyone's rights. As time went on some of her 'house husbands' would move out and find their own wives.

In the village where Mary Douglas lived the two oldest age-sets had each four village wives, the next only one. This reflects in part the influence of the Christian missions, whose converts, if they were men, neither joined in marrying village wives nor allowed their daughters to enter this status, and, if they were women, refused to be polyandrously married. Two granddaughters of village wives had been individually married. Dr Douglas calculates that in pagan days there were probably four village wives to an age-set.

The children of a village wife were sons of the village – of its men, and therefore not of any matrilineal descent group. The whole village counted as their father, though the men living with their mother had special responsibilities for them. Such a son could appeal to all his village-fathers for the raffia cloths he needed for marriage, to enter a cult association, to pay adultery damages. And when he died his funeral rites were performed at his mother's village by all the men who, as her husbands, were sons-in-law to that village.

Polyandry then seems to be ascribed to a number of different reasons in different places. The circumstances in which it is found are often present in societies that do not permit, much less enjoin it; so one cannot say that any particular conditions make it necessary. In Tibet it has the consequence of limiting the number of descendants to share an inheritance. It could, perhaps, be argued that the conditions of Tibet are so harsh, and its resources so limited, that large family units could not exist; this is in effect the argument advanced by Prince Peter of Greece in his *Study of Polyandry* (1963). But there are many kinds of harsh environment, and it is not altogether easy to see why this particular kind should necessitate polyandry. Nayar polyandry allows the matrilineal descent group to remain united instead of losing either sons or daughters when they marry;

but so do the Ashanti marriage arrangements. Lele polyandry is a resort for men who cannot obtain individual
wives; but there are many societies that do not practise polyandry although men have to wait to be married for some
years after they become adult. As for Kadara and Kagoro
polyandry, what shall one say? These peoples live in just the
same environment as many others who do not recognize
their custom of legalized 'wife-stealing'. Most British
anthropologists would, I think, see in these examples an argument against theories that social institutions are determined by the resources of the environment. There is an
American school of thought which seeks the explanation of
all social facts in the ratio between population and land area;
it would be interesting to hear their explanation of polyandry. It could of course be argued that, although the marriage of a woman simultaneously to more than one man is a
feature common to all these customs, the features which
differentiate them are more important.

Before leaving polyandry a final point must be noted: it is
not an *alternative* to polygyny. In all the societies mentioned
a man is permitted to have more than one wife (or, to ac-
commodate the Nayar, we might say to have socially approved children by more than one woman).

Plural Wives

To an anthropologist, particularly one whose main interests
are African, polygyny seems something to take for granted.
It is certainly much more familiar to laymen, perhaps because it has been so long regarded as the distinguishing mark
of paganism, and condemned by Christians as a denial of the
sanctity of the family and by feminists as degrading to
women. Moreover, many people associate polygyny with
Henry VIII. This is a great mistake. Henry VIII was a strict
monogamist, as the rules of European society required him
to be; he had to get rid of one wife before he could marry
another, and a turning point in the history of the English
church was reached when he decided that he must divorce

his first wife although the Pope, who claimed authority in such matters, would not allow it. People who think 'monogamy' ought to mean being married only once would use the term 'serial monogamy' to describe the marital experience of Henry VIII and of a number of our contemporaries in America and western Europe.

At the back of the condemnation of polygyny lies the notion that it is valued by the peoples who practise it as a form of sexual freedom for men. In missionary writings one finds references to backsliders who 'yield to temptation' and take a second wife, in contexts which suggest the same kind of 'yielding' as that of the man who takes too much to drink. But, if there is any question of yielding to temptation, it is the temptation of material advantage such as might lead a hitherto law-abiding citizen to become a spy or embezzle money; in other words, sexual variety is the least of the reasons why polygynous marriages are sought in societies which allow them.

Some of these have been mentioned incidentally in the chapter on marriage strategy, where the point was made that a marriage is an alliance, and that in societies where there are few bases for forming alliances it is as important to acquire affines as it is to acquire a spouse. Where positions of leadership are not hereditary (*ascribed*), they are attained by deploying resources to make alliances (as well as in other ways). Where they are hereditary, they are maintained, among other ways, by marriage alliances between the ruler and his henchmen. A Gisu chief in eastern Uganda, a Christian, said he could hardly do his job as a monogamist; 'he should marry several wives, then he has friends and can rule the people'. This man was not torn between self-restraint and temptation, but between the expectations of two types of authority, mission and government. This is the political aspect of polygyny.

Whereas Tibetan polyandry limits the members in a descent group, polygyny is the way to increase them, and is sought primarily to that end. Not every man can aspire to leadership, but anyone can hope to found a numerous lineage, and in his own lifetime to have sons to herd his cattle or work in his fields. A man whose wife bore no children or no sons would seek another for that reason (like Henry VIII). Plural wives are the mothers of these sons; they too work in the fields and produce the food that the household eats – sometimes all cultivation is women's work. Hospitality is a matter of food resources, above all of a sufficient surplus of the staple food to turn some of it into beer which can be offered to casual visitors. A house where beer can be expected is one where visitors congregate, and to establish one is a first step towards the winning of influence.

It used to be assumed that in a polygynous society *every* man had several wives, something which would not have been possible without a large surplus of women in the total population. So people further assumed that there was so much fighting in primitive conditions that a great many young men were killed before they could marry. Certainly some were, and some peoples devised the institution of 'ghost marriage' on their account. But this did not leave so many women that every man could marry more than one.

The real answer has been anticipated. Polygyny was the privilege of wealth as well as a means to wealth; it was a necessity of office as well as a way to attain office or leadership. In patrilineal societies it depended on resources for the payment of bridewealth. In matrilineal societies the payments required were less onerous, but the advantages of polygynous marriages were also less, since the offspring were not members of their father's lineage. In both types of society additional wives made a larger working team, producing more food and a surplus from which beer was brewed to offer to visitors. A village headman's obligations in hospitality depended in both on polygynous marriages, and since a headman was expected to live among his own descent group, he could have his wives with him even where this was not the general rule. Where the succession to headmanship was a matter of choice within a lineage, an aspirant could pave the way by marriage alliances with different factions. A reason given by the Plateau Tonga in Zambia for marrying two wives was that there a wife is responsible for brewing beer to sacrifice to her husband's ancestors, those of both his parents; sometimes, if a man was ill, the explanation given was that the two lines were annoyed at having only one woman to brew for both, and wished him to marry a second. There are also cases, in societies where the wife stays with her own kin after marriage, of what a former colleague of mine calls 'bicycle polygyny': a man has wives in two villages and commutes between them week by week; but this would be a temporary arrangement before the women's guardians gave him permission to take them away. Both in matrilineal and in patrilineal societies a widow is expected to go to a relative of her husband, and this, which is conceived in part at least as an obligation on such a man to care for her, accounts for some polygynous marriages.

The first man to make records of the incidence of polygyny in an African society was Livingstone, who in 1850 in a Tswana village found that out of 278 married men 94 had two wives, 25 had three, two had four.[2] Thus polygynists accounted for less than half the total. Census figures for the Pondo in South Africa in 1911 gave 10 per cent with two wives and only 2 per cent with more than two. Today no study of marriage in a polygynous society is considered to be complete if it does not include a census of the population on which it is based, preferably including such data as the proportion of adult men who are not married and the number of wives of men at different ages. The general conclusion is that at a given moment the majority of men in any society are married to only one wife, and that a very small proportion have more than two. High percentages of men with three or more wives have been recorded from the Tallensi in Ghana (9.6 per cent), the Yakö in eastern Nigeria (18 per cent), the pastoral Jie and Turkana in northern Kenya and Uganda (10 per cent and 28 per cent respectively) and the Arusha of Tanzania (21.5 per cent). As one would expect, the records show that older men have more wives; they have had time to accumulate resources for more bridewealth payments as well

2. Figures in I. Schapera, *Married Life in an African Tribe*, 1940.

as to inherit wives from their seniors. They have not necessarily deprived younger men for whom they are responsible
of the possibility to marry, but the demand for brides is increased by the fact that it comes from men already married
as well as from the unmarried, and polygyny can only be
maintained as long as girls are betrothed early, and married
as soon as they are nubile, while men may wait till they are
thirty or so. An eldest son is often married young because his
father is as anxious as he to ensure the continuance of his
line. If divorce is frequent a woman may marry more than
one man in succession (some might call this serial polyandry), and this increases the marriage opportunities for
men; but divorce is not an easy process where it is effected
by the repayment of bridewealth, and in many polygynous
societies it is rare.

Thus the spectacular harems of holders of political office
are the exception, not the rule, and indeed a little reflection
will show that nothing else could be possible. Nevertheless,
some societies so far idealize the large polygynous household
that they can state elaborate rules for the precedence of
wives and of the children of different wives, and for the
placing of their huts in the layout of the homestead.

Thus the Arusha in Tanzania, whose social structure is
based on a series of dual divisions, will tell you that a man
should create such a division between his sons by grouping
the children of different wives together. Once a man has two
wives, any later bride is allotted to the control of one or
other, and lives in this woman's hut until she has borne her
first child. The wives so linked have a special obligation to
cooperate in domestic work, and if the later married wife
dies the other should adopt her children. Gulliver's[3] account
gives actual examples of households with six wives, but even
for the Arusha with their high polygyny rate this must be
rare. Where there are only two wives it is everywhere normal
for them to co-operate and for their sons in the course of time
to head separate descent groups, and this must be the
common situation in Arusha. Again, the Nyakyusa, as has

3. P. H. Gulliver, *Social Control in an African Society*, 1963.

been mentioned, hold that a man should link his eldest son by the exchange of cattle received in bridewealth to the eldest son of each set of half-brothers. The statement implies the existence of a number of 'houses', but in fact there were rarely more than two in the homesteads that the Wilsons observed.

Ranking systems were traditionally characteristic of large, and therefore important, polygynous households among the south-eastern Bantu. The Xhosa gave special status to the first and second wives and allotted later ones to them as subordinates; the Swazi made three such divisions. A Swazi husband might also promote to the principal place a high-ranking woman married late in life. Tswana ranked all wives in order of marriage, but a girl who had been betrothed in infancy to a man yet unmarried would become his principal wife if he married her later than another woman; and so would a maternal cross-cousin.

Islam limits the number of simultaneous wives to four, and Koranic law stipulates, what is taken for granted in polygynous societies that do not have written laws, that the husband must give equal love and economic support to all. In a society dependent largely on subsistence production this implies sharing out the grain supply fairly between them (note that equality between wives does not necessarily create equality between children) and the fair distribution of meat, which men used to obtain by hunting. In rural Africa today fairness is rather a matter of the distribution of meat, clothes and household goods bought from the husband's wages; the wives there grow their own staple food.

But where women are not expected to contribute to subsistence and the household depends entirely on a cash income, equal distribution is a more difficult problem. For a man with middle-class aspirations to set up additional wives at the same level as the first is apt to become more and more difficult. Malays in Singapore said to Judith Djamour[4] that they could not afford polygyny on that basis; though

4. J. Djamour, *Malay Kinship and Marriage in Singapore*, 1959, pp. 83–5.

another view was that the provision of equal love would be even more difficult. Here there is a situation where polygyny has no economic advantages, and insofar as it enables a man already married to find a more congenial sexual partner, this can be achieved by a new marriage after the divorce which Islam makes easy. But Islam, at any rate as it is interpreted in some parts of the world, does not preclude the keeping of concubines, that is women whose status as such is recognized and who live in the household. Nadel, writing of the Fulani ruling class of Nupe Emirate in Nigeria, who are perhaps not the most orthodox of Muslims, observed that they divorced their older wives and married younger girls, still supporting the older women and giving them a home, or gave them in marriage to poor townsmen or peasants for a very low marriage payment.[5]

China, in pre-Republican days, could be said to combine the profession of monogamy with the practice of polygyny. That is to say, only one woman – naturally the one who was first brought into the house with all the correct ritual observances – was a man's wife in the full sense. But he was entitled to take a 'secondary wife' if the first did not bear children, and in practice this was done for many other reasons. This was a legally recognized relationship and was entered on publicly with appropriate ceremony. Concubines, as secondary wives are more commonly called in English writings, had a defined legal status. The first wife must always be accorded a superior position, however. She could not be repudiated without a formal divorce, whereas a concubine could be dismissed at any time.

One school of thought has seen in the superior position everywhere accorded to the first wife, and in the fact that second marriages are contracted with much less ceremony, and in Africa with a lower bridewealth, evidence that monogamy is man's 'natural' condition and polygyny a degeneration from a pristine state of innocence. But this view is not widely held, and one can suggest many other reasons. The first move from the unmarried to the married state is an

5. S. F. Nadel, *A Black Byzantium*, 1942, pp. 151-2.

irreversible change; it represents the attainment of full adult status and the beginning of socially recognized, as distinct from socially permitted, sexual activity. One wife is enough to set up a domestic unit; in a more complicated household there must be some authority in the performance of women's tasks, and this must be exercised by the senior. If the eldest son of the wife first married is to be the heir – particularly to political office – this is surely because in the normal course he will be senior to his brothers (and sometimes we find that the heir is not the son of the first wife but of a woman especially married to be the mother of the heir).

CHAPTER 10

'HONOUR'

THE point has been made often enough in this book that, as long as there is any question of arranging marriages to further the interests of persons other than the two partners, it is men who give women and not women who give men. Earlier chapters have shown how this affects the kind of payments or exchanges that accompany the conclusion of a marriage, and how rules laying down the appropriateness of marriages between persons in particular kin relationships can be interpreted as claims which men hold over particular women as brides. The perpetual minority of women, at least in theory always subject to male guardianship, is another aspect of this theme. Until the fairly recent period of emancipation, a woman has generally been assumed to be 'under the hand' of either a kinsman or a husband; only those who were able to hold substantial property in their own right, and not always they, were free from such control.

This principle does not only affect the formation of a household by the separation of a woman from her natal home; it also affects, to put the matter as crudely as possible, the condition in which she is delivered to her husband. Many peoples judge it to be of the utmost importance that a girl should remain a virgin until she is married, and many consider that if she does not, she brings disgrace upon her family as well as herself. If this were a universal attitude, it might be easier to make theories about it; one could argue that it was in some sense 'natural', as a missionary friend once tried to persuade me, citing in evidence an African girl who had enjoyed the freedom before marriage that her society allowed but was overcome with remorse when she came to be married. Insistence on virginity is by no means peculiar to Christians, nor do those who insist on it necessarily regard the loss of virginity as a sin; it may be conceived solely as an offence against the future husband. On the other hand it may, as in India, be held to have ritual consequences even more disastrous than those associated with it by Christians. In Africa some peoples make much of the preservation of virginity; others do not; the same is true of Polynesia. One generalization that can be made is that in all those societies that are commonly called 'the great civilizations' girls have been expected to be virgin at marriage. These are the societies that have founded empires and extended political control over wide areas and large populations; and in all of them, whether they are organized in descent groups or not, a child's status depends on a socially sanctioned relationship with his father. This latter fact may be correlated with an idea that a husband expects in marriage to gain control of his wife's *total* childbearing powers. Yet all husbands do not. Some payers of bridewealth are content to disregard the existence of earlier children of their brides, while others recognize as members of their lineage children whom their wives have borne before marriage. We do not know enough about the status of such women; whether they are married as second (polygynous) wives or by widowers. In either case less bridewealth would be given for them. We do not find many records of bridewealth-paying societies in which the loss of virginity as such is a bar to marriage, though a reputation for promiscuity would be. Where great store is set on virginity, the reasons given in different societies are not necessarily the same.

A second common characteristic of 'the great civilizations' is that they have all been highly stratified. They consist of conquerors and conquered, and their economies allow for wide differences in wealth and living standards. It would be easy to say, what is certainly true of some of them, that the dominant sections make play with their strict control of their girls as evidence of their superior morals. But then one finds that upward-moving groups such as the middle class in Victorian England claim that they are the moral superiors of the loose-living aristocracy. Perhaps there is no paradox; perhaps this assertion of 'bourgeois' morality went along with the final achievement of dominance by the bourgeoisie.

As was mentioned earlier in connection with endogamy, the restriction of marriage within a closed group is also a way of maintaining superiority. Caste endogamy in India has the effect of maintaining a social hierarchy. But the conception of the pollution entailed in contact with the less pure is not a mere rationalization. It is an essential part of Hindu religion. Caste membership is not hereditary merely in the legal sense. Legal inheritance rights are derived from one parent only – usually the father, occasionally the mother. But caste is a matter of one's bodily substance; it is actually derived from the bodies of one's parents, and it is the actual pollution of a forbidden sexual contact that is inherited by its offspring. Hence the importance attached to correct pedigree when a marriage is being negotiated.

Since it is the women who receive the male seed, it is they who can be defiled by union with men of lower caste and so be the source of pollution in their children, and it is towards their behaviour that the anxiety of their menfolk is directed. The anthropologist Nur Yalman finds in this attitude the explanation of various types of mock-marriage and other puberty rituals performed by the peoples of Ceylon and Southern India.[1] His Ceylonese informants told him that the honour and respectability of men is protected and preserved through their women. This is not a part of the world where offences against 'honour' are ideally wiped out in blood, and it is all the more interesting that Yalman found the word appropriate to translate the Ceylonese saying.

This is the source of the Indian view that a girl should be married before puberty, and thus formally attached to a man of the correct ritual status before there is any possibility of her incurring defilement by a polluting contact. As Yalman interprets the evidence it is the possible consequences of unchastity, and not unchastity as such, that concern the guardians of girls. Mock-marriages at puberty, such as those of the Nayars described in an earlier chapter, are performed where marriage does not give the husband any enduring

1. N. Yalman, 'On the Purity of Women in the Castes of Ceylon and Malabar', *Journal of the Royal Anthropological Institute*, 1963, p. 33.

rights over his wife; what they do is ritually to affirm the
association of a girl from the moment of her sexual maturity
with a man of the correct degree of purity to match her own.
Sometimes they simply associate her with a symbol of ritual
purity, as when the girl is 'married to a spear'. Yalman con-
trasts with these rites, which do no more than affirm (and
thus perhaps magically secure) the girl's freedom from sexual
pollution, the control of women practised by the Nambudiri
Brahmins of Malabar, who perform no such rites but secure
the same result in a severely practical manner by the strict
seclusion of all women before and after marriage.

Some puberty rituals include defloration, and some marriage rituals include defloration by some man in authority,
not the husband. This marks in the clearest possible way the
sanction of society for the entry on full sexual life. In Samoa,
when Margaret Mead forty years ago made her famous
study of adolescent girlhood, this had been forbidden by
American authorities but was a tradition recent enough to be
remembered (if not sometimes still practised). But here, as in
many parts of Africa, unmarried girls were not expected to
be without sexual experience. Sweethearting was permitted,
and, again as in parts of Africa, while the couple and their
kin gained prestige if a bride proved to be virgin, it was no
great loss if she did not. Ordinary folk could manage to avoid
the ceremony. But there were some girls who could not be
allowed to avoid it, nor to fail in the test. These were the
daughters of chiefs, and among them particularly any one
who was selected to be a 'ceremonial princess', to entertain
visitors to the village and pour the kava at gatherings of chiefs.
These girls were closely guarded, not allowed to sleep alone
or even go visiting in the daytime, and it is said that if one
failed the test of maidenhood her kinswomen would beat her
with stones, perhaps to death. 'The high chief', writes Margaret Mead, 'guards his daughter's virginity as he guards the
honour of his name, his precedence in the kava ceremony or
any other prerogative of his high degree.'[2] Again we have
the association of sexual restraint with high rank.

2. M. Mead, *Coming of Age in Samoa*, 1928; Pelican 1963, p. 84.

In Tikopia, another Polynesian island, a girl on attaining puberty fastens in her nose a shell ornament which proclaims that she is virgin. Men seek the favours of such a girl, and in the old days would proclaim success by smearing a drop of her blood on their forehead. When Firth was there in 1929 this custom had fallen into disuse, but a husband who found his wife to be virgin still had matter for boasting. 'He rejoices that he has been first to her, that when another man will go she will have been embraced. The man who was first at her will sit and laugh,' said one of Firth's informants.[3] Here too it was said that the daughters of chiefs remained virgin till their marriage, but it was not generally believed.

One finds a number of different attitudes among African peoples. Like the Samoans and Tikopians, and in striking contrast to those for whom 'honour' is the supreme value, many of them attach importance only to technical virginity. As was mentioned earlier, sex play between unmarried youths and girls is very widely permitted, provided it stops short of actual penetration, and parental supervision is limited to an examination of girls to see whether they have been deflowered (something evidently not practised in Polynesia). An exception is provided by the Ngoni aristocrats in Malawi, as they were observed by Margaret Read in 1938. The Ngoni of pre-colonial days were conquerors who travelled northwards from Zululand and eventually established a number of chiefdoms in the present-day Malawi and Zambia. Like most conquerors they emphasized the customs, particularly in the matter of sex, which differentiated them from their subjects, and contrasted the strict control they kept over their own girls with the early initiation into sex relations that their matrilineal neighbours approved.

It is among the south-eastern Bantu, from whom the Ngoni originally came, that most importance is attached to the preservation of technical virginity. These peoples, although they allowed and even institutionalized sweethearting between couples who need not eventually marry, did consider it disgraceful for a girl to be deflowered. Pedi girls

3. R. W. Firth, *We, the Tikopia*, 3rd ed. 1961, p. 519.

in the Transvaal would go into mourning for one of their number who lost her virginity, and Zulu women, perhaps with more realism, would go and shout their anger outside the seducer's house.

What the Ngoni did not take into account in their scorn for the matrilineal peoples was that they cut short the sex play between a betrothed boy and girl as soon as the girl reached puberty. Once she was capable of conception she must go through the initiation ritual which both blessed and permitted the bearing of children. In general where there is such a ritual, and it is practised among patrilineal as well as matrilineal peoples, the unpardonable offence is not the loss of virginity, or even pre-marital conception, but the bearing of children without this sanction. The most dramatic account of the reaction to this offence comes from the Kipsigis, a patrilineal people in Kenya.[4] To them it is more a sin against the spirits than an affront to a potential husband. The trouble is not that the girl or her parents are put to shame by her sinful act, but that the whole community is contaminated by its consequence, the appearance of a child whose life has not been blessed in advance by the necessary ritual. The unsanctioned child makes its mother unclean, so that unless she is ritually purified, she will never be able to bear another; and this, and not any conception of unchastity in a moral sense, is what debars her from marriage. The child must be born in the bush, where its uncleanness cannot harm the homesteads; and it should be smothered at once, so that it can be considered as never having lived. If this is done, and the mother ritually cleansed, she can return to normal life. Colonial rule punished infanticide, and the Christian missions adopted these unauthorized children; but their mothers then were disgraced and could never marry.

According to Peristiany no disgrace attached to an unmarried mother whose child was born after she was initiated; on the contrary, a prospective husband would be glad of the evidence of her fertility and would make the child his own by a bridewealth payment. This attitude has

4. J. G. Peristiany, *The Social Institutions of the Kipsigis*, 1939.

also been said to characterize urbanized Africans in places as far apart as Ghana and South Africa.

Other African peoples have different views, however. It is again among the south-eastern Bantu that unmarried mothers were traditionally treated with the greatest severity. A Kgatla (Tswana) girl who became pregnant was ostracized by her friends, and the neighbours gathered outside her house and sang obscene songs; in the past her child might have been put to death. A Xhosa girl in the Transkei in South Africa could never hope to marry if she bore a child out of wedlock, but she was accorded a recognized, if inferior status, and might continue to bear children while living in her parents' home. Many Xhosa girls took care not to become pregnant until an age when they seemed unlikely to be sought in marriage; it is where the practice of partial intercourse has been given up that young girls bear pre-marital children.

Among the more permissive Nuer, an unmarried mother suffers no penalty beyond a certain loss of esteem. Some girls bear children by several lovers in succession, and according to Evans-Pritchard the Nuer do not stigmatize them as immoral but recognize that they are 'temperamentally unfitted for married life'.[5] But he also says that 'no respectable girl wants to be an unmarried mother', and that girls who have too many sweethearts, even if they do not have children, are not sought in marriage. A girl's brother depends on her marriage cattle to provide his own bridewealth, and one cannot suppose that such a brother bears his disappointment with beautiful meekness.

Many African societies, nevertheless, emphasize virginity in marriage ritual. Possibly this parallels the defloration rites mentioned earlier, with their symbolism of entry on a new status in which sexual fidelity, as well as accessibility, to the husband is the most important obligation. This is perhaps implied in Evans-Pritchard's comment on the Nuer consummation ceremony, which is an indispensable part of the marriage ritual. In it the bride is expected to simulate reluc-

5. *Kinship and Marriage among the Nuer*, 1951, p. 53.

tance and inexperience although the chance that these reactions are genuine is remote in the extreme. 'I doubt,' he says, 'whether any girl in Nuerland goes to her husband a virgin', and he adds: 'Maidenhood is a social, not a physical, state'; and the same ceremony is performed in just the same way if the girl is pregnant or is being married for the second time.

Elsewhere great interest is shown in the virginity of a bride, and it is celebrated with rejoicing when the case allows, and often acknowledged by a gift to her mother in gratitude for her strict bringing-up; and sometimes a bride who is found not to be virgin meets with opprobrium.

But even if many African peoples are not greatly perturbed by the knowledge that many brides are often not virgins, one cannot ignore the fact that the matter is tested in many marriage rituals, that when a girl passes the test it is ground for rejoicing and sometimes for making a special present to her mother, and that her failure is sometimes expressly noted.

For example, at a Nyakyusa marriage ritual, which is held as soon as possible after the bride's first menstruation, a bull, additional to the bridewealth cattle, is given if examination shows her to be a virgin (or if the husband asserts that he has himself deflowered her). The bull is brought to the girl's home before the examination, and when the favourable report is announced women of the girl's lineage rush through the homestead shouting 'It's ours, it's ours!' If she had been found to be not a virgin the bull would have been returned.

The Vugusu of western Kenya required a man to deflower his bride in public – until, some forty years ago, they began to find that too many girls were not virgins. Some of their neighbours, and some West African peoples too, would send a special present to the mother of a virgin bride to thank her for the care she had taken of her daughter. As expressions of disapproval in the contrary event one might quote the Yoruba, where a bride's mother expected a present of cowries in any case, but was given inferior ones if her daughter was found to have been deflowered; or the Hausa, where the disappointed husband would come outside his house and break a pot in sight of the passers-by. In the Nuba hills in the west of Sudan a bride who had lost her virginity could be repudiated, or would be beaten and abused by her husband.

African girls then are not expected to be 'innocent' of any knowledge of sexual matters. They know just what they are doing and how far it is safe to go, and what is important to themselves and to their kin is to avoid making themselves unmarriageable. Pride in the close control of girls and in virginity for its own sake is rare, despite the Ngoni example. There is nowhere a belief that the loss of virginity is displeasing to supernatural beings; what offends them is for children to be born before the ritual of initiation, and this ritual blesses and authorizes not sexual congress as such, but fruitful congress. For the married there are many occasions of supernatural punishment for transgression; a difficult birth is ascribed to the woman's infidelity, and it is believed that the child cannot be born until she has confessed the name of her lover; a husband's infidelity in particular circumstances, notably when he is away from home and when his wife is pregnant, is believed to make his children sick.

Of these societies, then, one could say that punishment for sexual transgressions, unless they are discovered *in flagrante*, is in the main left to supernatural beings. The family of a marriageable girl are concerned that she should not behave in such a way as to be considered unmarriageable, and after she is married her husband controls her as far as he is able, partly by exercising an acknowledged right to beat her if she fails in any of her obligations.

But in many parts of the world the sexual reputation of a woman before and after marriage is held to reflect on the standing of both her own family and her husband's. Where this is so, any suggestion that a sister or a wife has behaved in too free a manner is an insult to be avenged, and if a girl actually loses her virginity, or a wife betrays her husband, the ideally appropriate reaction is to kill both the woman and her seducer. These principles are part of a code of honour with wider implications, which extends into the field of the blood-feud or revenge murder, as well as into that of the duel as the reaction to an insult of any kind. It provides themes for melodrama, and for self-righteous moralizing by the unromantic denizens of a world where violence is admired only in the furtherance of collective aims.

Wherever people claim to adhere to standards that involve such dramatic consequences, closer study generally reveals that the extreme course may be admired but is not always taken. Girls who are 'dishonoured' in fact go on living, and may even find husbands, if not very satisfactory ones. Blind eyes may be turned, or some form of token revenge accepted, such as the duel in which pistols are fired in the air.

The question that is interesting from the point of view of the present discussion is what in fact depends on the preservation of honour, or on its loss. How far do men actually go towards the ideal to which they all give lip-service? Does this vary between societies all of which assert the honour code, between social classes in these societies or between individuals?

A number of such societies have recently been the subject of work by anthropologists. They include the Pathans of the Swat Valley, described by F. Barth,[6] and countrymen or small-town dwellers in Greece and southern Italy. The Pathans in their remote valley of the Himalayan foothills are the dominant population of an area where there is no central authority – where might is right in the sense that, although people subscribe to a common code of conduct, the best way to secure rights which are recognized, or to prevail where rights are disputed, is to command more force than your adversary.

Competing chiefs, therefore, must gather followers, if possible at the expense of their rivals, and one way to do so is to have a reputation for courage in the defence of honour. For a man honour has as many aspects as there are words or

6. F. Barth, *Political Leadership among Swat Pathans*, 1959.

actions that can be interpreted as offensive, but one of the most grievous offences is to imply that he cannot or does not effectively control the women for whom he is responsible. Hence it behoves these women to avoid any behaviour that could give rise to comment of this kind. Barth in his short discussion of this subject does not record any theory that a woman who offends must be punished with death. He does observe that a man who wishes to preserve his honour is expected to kill the seducer of his sister or wife; and that a man who divorced his wife would be suspected of doing so because she was guilty of adultery with someone he was afraid to attack. Also, that the pursuit of blood-revenge is not a continuous process like war; if nobody doubts the wronged man's courage, he can await a suitable opportunity without losing face, and feuds can last for years with no more than one or two homicides in a generation. Honour is what other people are willing to allow you; it is in the eye of the beholder. If your honour-rating is high enough people will hesitate to insult you.

Honour, then, is the amount of esteem that others accord you, but it is not measured on a fixed scale. Circumstances alter cases, and a change in circumstances may alter the honour-rating of persons involved in the same case. If group loyalties come into play insiders and outsiders will be differently judged. An incident told me by David Brooks from the Bakhtiari in the mountains of Iran illustrates these points. A man, X, who lived near a road a long way from a village, made an income by prostituting his wife to passers-by, in itself a thoroughly dishonourable thing to do. One of these passers-by was a government servant, Y, who often had to visit the area; he became fond of the girl and persuaded the husband (by paying a sum of money) to let him be the girl's only lover. This again was not perhaps very honourable. After a few months the girl ran away from her husband and turned up at the young man's office in Isfahan, and he decided to marry her. This was such an outrage to the husband, dishonoured though he was by his own conduct, and to his tribesmen that neither Y nor his bride dared enter X's tribal area. When the young man at last had to go there on government work, he had to run for his life. For a year he was in danger from any member of the tribe whom he might meet. However, a marriage was arranged. Y was asked to pay compensation for abduction, but argued that it was he who had behaved with honour in rescuing the girl. Other tribes, always ready to score points in the honour game, pretended to think it was the custom in X's tribe for men to prostitute their wives, and called them by derogatory names. There was no doubt that X had brought shame on them in the eyes of outsiders. Soon after the marriage Y was badly injured in a road accident. Some held that this was the revenge of X's tribe, but others said it was God's punishment for his dishonourable act in paying for the girl in the first place, especially as he seemed likely to lose his looks. But he recovered, and did not lose his looks. Nothing succeeds like success. Again he became an honourable man who had shown courage in standing by the girl, resourcefulness in protecting her from her vengeful tribesmen, and so on.

In stratified societies concern for honour, in which female honour is usually an essential element, is claimed as a characteristic of the dominant section. But the same concern is to be found among people who are not in a position to dominate anybody, for example the Sarakatsan shepherds of north-western Greece[7] or the peasants of southern Italy. In their eyes a girl can indeed be dishonoured by the mere suspicion that she is not a virgin, and a woman's honour, unlike a man's, cannot be retrieved once it has been lost. The shotgun marriage is the answer in a society where the most important issue is the legitimization of children. For the Sarakatsani this is no answer. A dishonoured girl can hope at best to marry a widower or a man of low standing; and it is also their belief that her daughters inherit her shamelessness.

Unlike most of the peoples discussed in this book, the Sarakatsani attach as much importance to male as to female virginity. Many African peoples regard sexual intercourse as

7. J. Campbell, *Honour, Family and Patronage*, 1964.

in some sense dangerous, perhaps polluting, so that it is forbidden to people who are engaged in hazardous enterprises, and often to those who are about to perform rituals of various kinds. The Sarakatsani go further, and, with St Paul, consider it as shameful in itself, necessary though it is for the continuance of the family on which they set so much store. It is the evil nature of women which, in their eyes, tempts men as it has ever since Eve tempted Adam. So women are not frail creatures in danger from predatory males, but snares of the Devil, and it is incumbent on them to do what they can to neutralize their inherently dangerous qualities. They must dress in a manner that conceals their shape, must move slowly with eyes on the ground, not answer men's greetings. Before a girl is married she should spend her time at home weaving clothes for her dowry; if possible she should not be sent to fetch water or collect firewood. As a wife these will be among her most arduous tasks, but they will be done in the company of other wives. Only after she has a married son is she allowed a little freedom from the formal rules of modest conduct.

To the Sarakatsani, as to other southern European populations, honour as a quality attaches primarily to an individual, but through him (or her) to his family. The behaviour of every member can affect the esteem given to the family as a unit. If any one of them conspicuously falls short of the ideal standard of behaviour, all are dishonoured. For a woman to fail in sexual modesty dishonours her father and brothers (and indeed her future offspring), and for them to fail in the appropriate response compounds the dishonour. Among Sarakatsani the family is the only unit within which people expect to count on total solidarity. Outside it is a world whose hostility is tempered only by the less compelling obligations of kinship. A family moves as a unit on the honour scale. It is easier to fall than to rise; the maintenance of honour, rather than its increase, is every man's pre-occupation. So if a woman willingly surrenders her honour, this is a 'betrayal from within', an ultimate treachery, a preference for an outsider, or for pleasure, over the

most sacred ties. Along with the theory of women's natural
frailty, or worse, this is enough to explain the jealous watch
kept over them, and the idea that to succeed in preserving
this, its most vulnerable aspect, is the ultimate test of
honour.

John Davis[8] develops this theme in a discussion of a hill
town in southern Italy. In his view, although 'honour' is the
object of competition, it is something more. It is for every
man or woman the sum total of all comments that could be
made on their performance of the roles allotted to them, and
this sum, if it could be expressed numerically, would represent the credit attached to a man's 'word of honour'.
Honour is, Davis puts it, essentially a matter of family
duties, because outside the family no holds are barred; again
this expresses in a slightly different way Campbell's con-
tention that the family is the only group whose members
should be able absolutely to count on one another. But the
evaluation of honour in Pisticci is not confined to the key
qualities of courage and chastity; it refers to success or failure in the whole gamut of activities of family life. An
honourable woman is not only a faithful wife; she is also a
good housekeeper, and she restrains her husband from wast-
ing his money on drink. In the never-ending assessment of
honour in which Pisticcesi are engaged, dramatic tales of
killing for the sake of honour had a relatively small place.
Although men would assert that they accepted this obligation and would not hesitate to fulfil it if the occasion
arose, they could remember very few cases; and there were
more known cases of adultery and seduction. The reason is
that in fact the rules of sexual honour are not inflexible, and
that in Pisticci, as in some more sophisticated societies,
though not among the Sarakatsani, a girl's lost honour can
be restored if her seducer marries her. While negotiations are
going on her brothers threaten her lover, and only if he
refuses to marry her is it thought necessary to wipe out the
family shame in his blood. Even then, moreover, the code

8. J. Davis, 'Honour and Politics in Pisticci', *Proceedings of the Royal
Anthropological Institute*, 1969.

may not always require it. The reason is one that is again not peculiar to Pisticci. Honour, as has been indicated, is not an absolute quality but a basis for ranking; one family has more, another less. The less honourable are expected to put up with slights from the more honourable; this is the practical expression of their inferiority in honour. The gay deceiver, then, finds his partner among his honour inferiors, to use Davis's convenient words; and it is only when the injured party does not recognize the other as his superior that the question of vengeance arises. Adultery in modern Italy is a crime, and its victim can threaten a court case and demand satisfaction in money. Hence a woman's adultery can be condoned with the explanation 'she does it to feed her family' – 'She was poor but she was honest' with a new twist.

I described Pisticcesi as people who are not in a position to dominate anyone. As a class they are not; they belong to the lowest stratum of Italian society. But each man of them is seeking to establish and maintain for his family a reputation for honour which will not only protect them as a group from the worst forms of slight but will enable him as a man to be regarded as trustworthy; to obtain credit in the narrower sense because he is held to be honourable in the wider. Perhaps it is not logical to argue that a man will keep his word because he is known to keep his daughters in order, but that is how the Pisticcesi see it.

I quote a final instance from southern Italy of the association between male honour and female virginity simply because it is so recent, having been reported in *The Times* in April 1970. A man who discovered on his wedding night that his bride was not the virgin she claimed to be demanded a separation on the ground that she had 'knowingly committed the crime of causing him grave dishonour'. A court in Naples granted the separation. His wife successfully appealed to a higher court, who held that if anyone had dishonoured the husband it was the unknown man who earlier seduced his wife-to-be. The husband took the case yet higher, now arguing that a concealment of the truth such as his wife's 'gravely injured the sentiments of mutual trust, loyalty and honesty on which conjugal affection should be based'. Accordingly it was his wife and none other who had dishonoured him.

Journalists, unlike anthropologists, cannot pursue their stories in a context of time or place, and the source of this story does not tell us what the upshot was, nor yet what the couple and the woman's near kin were doing during the *eight years* that the case was argued in the courts. As the story is told it seems that the wife herself and not her brothers publicly bore the brunt of the husband's indignation; also that only the husband, and not the wife's family, was held to be dishonoured. How much must be hidden behind this brief report. Is it an illustration of a new attitude towards 'honour'? Or a set of facts the meaning of which is distorted when they are out of context?

Where men expect or hope to find virgin brides, the question how often the ideal is achieved must depend on two factors: the age of the girl at betrothal, and the care with which her movements are watched. A girl once promised is sexually bound to her husband. This is the case in Africa as well as in the stricter societies; his right to compensation for an adultery begins from the time of betrothal. An obligation to a designated man is a stronger argument for chaste behaviour than an abstract principle would be. Of one Indian village an anthropologist has written that the essential for the preservation of honour is to contract the girl before there can be any question of loss of virginity. What happens after she is 'properly married' may be the concern of her husband but it does not injure 'family honour'. That, the supreme value, is protected at the cost of breaking the law against marriage of girls under fourteen. Even here there are sometimes unsanctioned pregnancies; then if the girl cannot be quickly married to her lover, she may be taken as a second wife by the husband of one of her sisters, or by some boy whose family cannot afford the expense of a properly ostentatious wedding.

In China, although the idea of the unblemished gift is

absent, the expectation that the bride be virgin is equally
strong. This is one of the matters that a go-between should
inquire into with the appropriate discretion. A Chinese
anthropologist, Hsu,[9] tells us that if a girl who had not yet
been betrothed was found to be unchaste she could only
hope to marry in some place far from her home where
she was not known. But he adds that if her misdemeanour
was only found out after she was married, the loss of honour
to the family she had joined, if they made this public by
sending her away, would be greater than they could face. So
she would stay in her husband's family, to which she now
wholly belonged, enduring their contempt and dislike.

So it may be truer to say that high-class families set store
by an appearance of strict standards than that they treat
lapses with the severity that they logically deserve. This is
what is often called, in another context, 'Victorian hypoc-
risy'. A student of society might say that the stricter the code
professed, the more necessary it becomes to turn a blind eye
to lapses if life is not to become impossible. Also, with the
example of Pisticcesi before us, we cannot say that it is *only*
the members of upper classes who pursue honour. If one
takes the view that all men strive for prestige in one sphere
or another, we might argue that a peasant population such
as the Pisticcesi, who have not yet been effectively sucked
into the competition for affluence that characterizes the industrialized world, find in honour the most significant form
of achievement.

However, the control of women's behaviour, whether as
maidens or wives, is certainly correlated in part with status.
It is in Muslim and Hindu societies that a woman is expected
to be concealed from the gaze of any man other than her
husband. For this to be possible a family must be able to
employ servants on the tasks that fall to the wives of poorer
men – working in the fields, fetching water and firewood,
trading in the market. In some African Muslim societies, the
Hausa for example, there is a marked difference between the
secluded life of well-to-do wives and the freedom of peasant

9. F. L. Hsu, *Under the Ancestors' Shadow*, 1949, p. 98.

women, who are no more strictly hidden from public sight than are their pagan sisters. But there can be cultural arrangements which enable women to do peasant work and still meet the requirements of concealment. Barth[10] describes the life of women in Kohistan, where, he says, people are very much stricter in these matters than most of their neighbours. No girl over ten years old must show her face to any man outside her nearest kin. A woman may go out with her husband, but if they meet some other man she must cover her head and face completely and hide behind a bush until he is out of sight. If a man passes a band of women who are working in the fields they too cover their heads, stop working and squat under the shelter of the wall till he has gone by. Of course a properly brought up man does not try to penetrate their concealment, and he is expected not to pass close by the place where the group of women are.

In one way and another, all these attitudes are concerned with the child-bearing capacity of women and the assignment of their offspring to the appropriate group. In ascetic religions such as Hinduism and Christianity there is in addition the belief that restraint as such is meritorious, and the idea that we find among the Sarakatsani that women are inherently dangerous to men and must on that account be kept under strict control may be more widespread; it is striking in how many myths woman's disobedience is held to have been the cause of the separation of men from gods and to have brought death into the world. The Pisticcesi show us that the notion of 'honour' is not as exclusively concerned with sexual conduct as we may have been inclined to assume; nevertheless, sexual conduct plays a large part in it, and a very fundamental element in honour is the control of women so as to secure that there shall be no bastards in the family. All these ideas arise essentially from the need to ascribe an unambiguous status to every new member born into a society, and it is when ascribed status begins to lose importance that they can be interpreted, and rejected, as expressions of exaggerated puritanism.

10. F. Barth, *Indus and Swat Kohistan*, 1956.

CHAPTER II

THE TERMINATION OF MARRIAGE

AT the time when demands began to be made in England for a relaxation in the laws of divorce, the ideal of indissoluble marriage was commonly held to be an expression of the sexual puritanism of the Christian Church. In fact it is by no means confined to Christendom, and societies which permit divorce nevertheless regard it as desirable that marriages should endure. Where they are made, as is described in Chapter 5, for the sake of an advantageous alliance between families and descent groups, their promoters naturally do not wish to see them dissolved. This applies particularly to the political marriages of nomad herdsmen such as the Bedouin, through which one group gains access to water or pastures controlled by another. Even where divorce is frequent, marriage procedures and ritual, as well as people's comments on one another's behaviour, generally make it clear that lasting unions are valued. An earlier chapter mentioned the attitude of the Ngoni of Zambia, for whom a union entered upon without formalities is called a 'poorly-fixed marriage' as long as it is doubtful whether it will last, but imperceptibly attains the status of a 'marriage' if it proves to be stable. An anthropologist writing of a society, the Gonja, in which women very frequently leave their husbands for other men, remarks: 'It seems likely that for even minimal stability the actors must assume that, at least in *their* (own) case, it will last.'[1]

This same anthropologist remarks, however, that if one observes in any given society that marriages tend to be of short duration, one need not take this as a sign of some kind of social breakdown. Many questions need to be asked. What

1. E. Goody, 'Separation and Divorce among the Gonja', in *Marriage in Tribal Societies*, ed. M. Fortes, 1962, p. 53.

kind of relations between spouses are expected? The answer
will depend in part, though not entirely, on the questions discussed in an earlier chapter: What rights does a husband
gain in the marriage contract? What is the marital status of
a widow – not an empty question, as the discussion of bridewealth has shown. What are the reasons for a couple to separate? Who is most likely to initiate the separation, husband
or wife? Are the recognized procedures for ending a marriage difficult or easy? How often are they resorted to? (The
answers to the last two questions do not necessarily coincide.)
Is separation more common at one stage in married life –
say, before children have been born or after a woman's
child-bearing years are over – than at others? Is there some
relation between marital stability and social status? What
religious ideas are associated with marriage?

Marriage can be terminated in other ways than by
divorce. A couple may separate, and so cease to play the
roles of husband and wife, without taking the formal steps
required to end the marriage. Such a separation without a
formal divorce may be held to free them – or the woman in a
polygynous society – for a new marriage. On the other hand,
the union created by marriage may be held to last even
beyond death; this is a rule that applies more often to wives
than to husbands.

To a large extent the expectations of different societies in
these matters are a matter of the significance of marriage in
determining the status of children. In many western countries, when a couple divorce the courts decide who is to have
'custody of the children'. For practical purposes this means
which parent they will live with, and obviously it is this
parent who will have most influence on their upbringing.
The question which one will benefit from their contribution
to the housekeeping when they are old enough to earn may
weigh with some parents, but it does not play a large part
in the decisions of judges.

Some anthropologists write of the 'custody' of the children of a divorced couple in non-industrial societies, but it
might give a more accurate impression to talk of their status,

as members of a lineage or joint family. In these societies, in contrast to those of the 'western' world, this status is significant for a man all through his life, and for a woman at least until she is married and often after.

So we come directly to the contrast between patrilineal and matrilineal descent and their respective consequences for the nature of marriage. It is in patrilineal societies that a woman bears children for another lineage and among those who pay bridewealth in cattle we find that her children belong to her husband's lineage no matter who begets them and that she remains his wife even when he is dead. As was indicated in reference to the Nuer, this does not always debar her from living with a man of her choice, someone other than her husband's heir. Schapera, however,[2] tells us of the Kgatla of Botswana that a widow was traditionally expected to choose from her dead husband's kinsmen in a public ceremony, and if she refused them all they would be offended and might take her to the chief's court. Only if none of them wanted her was she free to take a lover, and he must be a man from the same 'ward' (a village, or a section of a town under its own headman). Otherwise she might go home to her own kin, have them return the bridewealth, and marry again. Thus she would be divorced after the death of her husband. If she stayed among his kin it would not be correct to say that she became the wife of one of them; she was still married to her dead husband, for whom his kinsman acted as proxy. Perhaps the stricter rules of the Kgatla are connected with the fact that lineage kin there lived as a compact group, as they do not among the Nuer.

Indissoluble Marriage

The Hindu conception of marriage as an indissoluble union is expressed, like the Christian, in terms of its sacramental quality. There is no provision here, as there is with the payers of bridewealth, for a divorce which would set a widow free, though a widower needs no divorce from his

2. I. Schapera, *A Handbook of Tswana Law and Custom*, 1938, pp. 164–7.

dead wife, but is expected to re-marry. At the time of the Vedic writings – the original source of Hindu law, which all the later stages claimed only to be clarifying – that is, some time before 1600 B.C., it seems that widows were often, perhaps usually, re-married to a brother or other kinsman of the husband. But the prevalent view today, which was already established by the beginning of the Christian era, is that a woman once married is married once for all. The kindling of the sacred fire during the marriage ritual marks the beginning of rites to be performed daily by the couple for the rest of their lives. In fact the husband performs the rites, but the wife must be present. Their relationship indeed can be well expressed in Milton's famous line: 'He for God only, she for God in him'. The woman is expected to merge her identity in her husband's, and not to wish to live after him. A truly devoted wife used to be called a *sati*, and the final proof of her devotion was to throw herself on his funeral pyre and be consumed along with his body. This, it was believed, would bring joy to her in the next world and glory to her memory, and, according to some versions of Hindu religion, would help to save her husband from hell. She became a sort of saint, and people prayed to her for blessings. The act also has the name *sati*. It was never universally approved, but in Bengal in particular it was very prevalent among the higher castes in the early nineteenth century, and it was clearly not always an act of free choice. A British law, which had the support of the famous Ram Mohun Roy, founder of the Brahma Samaj, made *sati* illegal in 1829. Yet it has not entirely died out; there have been a dozen known cases since India became independent.

But the fate of widows is not happy. Since a girl on marriage is transferred wholly to her husband's family, a widow cannot return to her own home. She must remain with them and depend on them for support, but she no longer has the status of a wife, and is further believed to be a source of bad luck, so that she must keep away from any auspicious occasion such as a family ritual. Widows must shave their heads and may not wear shoes. Where the strict rule is followed, even a young girl who has been betrothed in child-hood must enter this status if her husband dies before she has joined him. A widower on the other hand is expected to find a new wife to enable him to perform the daily domestic ritual and to bear him children. And although he may not divorce his wife, a man is allowed to 'supersede' her by taking another if she fails to bear him children. The social reform wing of the Indian National Congress advocated the re-marriage of widows from 1885, and Indian statute law authorized it as early as 1856; but it is still confined almost entirely to the educated minority.

The Chinese, too, hold that a woman should be the wife of one man only, and express this attitude by setting up mem-orials to widows who remain chaste. But, great as is the im-portance of the lineage in Chinese society, they do not believe that a widow who wishes to continue sexual life should bear children to another member of her husband's lineage. On the contrary, she is considered to have been so completely absorbed into that lineage that marriage to a member other than her husband would be incestuous, and she has also become a part of it in the sense that, if she re-marries, it is they and not her original family who arrange the marriage. Like the Hindu woman, her only home is that of her husband; although she is not cut off from contact with her kin she should not return to live with them. But widow-hood is not in itself a despised status; on the contrary. A widow with young children might take on the management of her husband's estate and hold on to it after her sons had grown up, and Chinese history remembers the widowed mothers of more than one famous man. Ideally a widow should not re-marry, and those who do so may not be re-corded in the genealogies that are preserved in the lineage ancestral halls; but in fact they do marry again.

Whether a Chinese wife could be divorced is open to doubt. The evidence from different areas indicates that the rules were not the same all over that vast empire, but at any rate the books do not describe divorce procedures. Women did leave their husbands if they were dissatisfied, and go

home for long visits or for good. But in one respect a
woman's ties with her own home were permanently severed
by marriage; it could no longer be the home of her spirit
after she died. So if she broke her contact with her husband's
family her ghost would have to wander homeless. For protection against this fate, and doubtless also for other reasons,
widows, women who had left their husbands, and a few who
did not wish to marry, lived in 'old maids' houses', of which
there were many. Such a woman's name would be recorded
there on wooden tablets like those set up for ancestors, and
she was commemorated on the anniversary of her death.[3]

Divorce in Africa

Islam allows divorce, and so do the majority of societies in
Africa south of the Sahara. That is to say there is a recognized way of terminating a marriage and freeing the woman
to enter into a legal union with another man. I describe the
effect of divorce in this way because where polygyny is recognized a man does not have to dissolve one marriage before
contracting another.

Many writers have enumerated 'grounds for divorce' in
African societies, but it should be understood that these are
not conditions which must be satisfied before a couple can be
released from their obligations. One can only speak of
grounds for divorce in that sense where a divorce requires
the formal sanction of judicial authorities and the conditions for it are stated in a written law. Otherwise one
cannot go beyond recording typical arguments which in
different societies have been held to justify a wife in leaving
her husband or a husband in driving away his wife.

Divorce procedures, again, may be easy or difficult to
carry out. The Muslim husband only has to say to his wife 'I
divorce you' three times and need give no reason; this statement, taken literally, is the classic example of easy divorce. A
husband who has paid bridewealth may only have to ask his

3. M. Freedman, *Chinese Lineage and Society*, 1966, p. 56, quoting C. K.
Yang, *A Chinese Village in Early Communist Transition*, 1959.

wife's kinsmen to return it, but it is likely to be difficult for them to produce the appropriate number of cattle, and it may take some time. The charade of the injured spouse who must qualify for release by cutting off relations with the erring partner, and at the same time not admit to any feeling that it would be a good thing to end the marriage, used to make divorce a complicated matter in the English courts.

But one cannot draw conclusions about the frequency of divorce from the simplicity or otherwise of the procedure. While it is likely that divorce rates will be high when procedures are simple, one must also ask how much importance is attached in different societies to the continuation of a marriage, and whether the idea that a family can be dishonoured by the behaviour of its women is a counterweight to formal ease of divorce. One must also ask how often, and in what circumstances, in different societies couples separate without a formal divorce.

Earlier chapters have discussed the different significance of marriage in patrilineal and matrilineal societies. In the former, marriage enables a man to attach to his line of descent the children whom his wife bears; in the latter, children take their descent from their mothers, so that a man looks to his sister for heirs. In these societies, there is not the same desire to attach a woman to one husband and one descent line. The woman's closest ties remain with her own lineage, and a divorce is usually effected by her guardians dismissing her husband. It is generally accepted that divorce is more common in matrilineal than in patrilineal societies, but they nevertheless have institutions to deal with marital quarrels and to seek a reconciliation of the spouses. In Malawi a marriage is agreed upon in discussions between two representatives of the kin of either party. Ideally these should be a mother's brother and a sibling of each. It is the nomination of these 'marriage sponsors' or 'marriage guardians', as they have been called by different anthropologists, that gives formal sanction to the marriage. Complaints by either spouse against the other should be taken to his own marriage sponsors, who then discuss them with their opposite numbers. In some of these societies (e.g. Yao and Cewa), where the rule is for the man to spend the first years of marriage at the home of his wife's parents, they keep a close watch over his treatment of her. When the time comes for him to ask their permission to take her away, they consider whether he can be relied on to treat her properly, and answer accordingly. If they refuse, he may leave his wife, or she and her kin may make this crucial moment the occasion to dismiss him.

Among the matrilineal peoples of Zambia a final payment is made at this time. It is not altogether clear from the accounts of anthropologists whether it is the payment itself, or the establishment of an independent household which the payment authorizes, that is held to make divorce a more weighty matter after the marriage has reached this stage. They agree that up to that point a husband can be dismissed with little excuse and no appeal, whereas after it there is argument as to who is at fault and as to the return of the payment. But it seems that the latter point has gained significance only since the amount has increased along with the circulation of money.[4] The Plateau Tonga hold that by accepting the payment the wife's kin undertake a new responsibility to keep the marriage in being by exerting their influence on her. They may refuse it either because they dislike the husband or because they cannot control their kinswoman. This need not result in the separation of the couple, but since the marriage payments have not been completed they will strictly speaking not be legally married, and it will be open to the woman's kin to take her back and marry her to another man.

Is divorce, then, 'more' or 'less difficult' according as it does or does not entail the return of a marriage payment? At one time anthropologists made much of the argument that bridewealth was a guarantee of the stability of marriage because the difficulty of returning it was an incentive to the receivers to keep their womenfolk faithful to their husbands.

4. See e.g. A. I. Richards, *Bemba Marriage and Present Economic Conditions*, 1940.

It has been shown in earlier chapters that, if it has such an effect at all, this is by no means its main significance. Symbolically, rather than as a kind of bail or security, it binds those who have received it to an interest in the marriage, but this has two sides; among some peoples a wife who leaves her husband has a claim on the protection of any kinsman who has received a part of her bridewealth.

Under colonial rule chiefs' courts were given authority to decide civil cases, subject to the supervision of European officials who were concerned to maintain standards of justice that conformed to their values. To this end they sought to record customary law or to get anthropologists to do so, and in the final years before independence, judicial advisers were appointed in the British territories with the function, among others, of promoting consistency in the decisions of different courts. All this has produced, in the writings of anthropologists and elsewhere, lists of 'grounds for divorce' accepted by different peoples, which are in fact lists of the reasons for seeking divorce that have been considered sufficient, first by the kinsmen of a couple and then, if the question arose, by a chief in court. Cases taken to court are rarely concerned with divorce *per se*, rather with quarrels about amounts to be returned or damages to be paid, the latter a new notion that chiefs' courts introduced under colonial rule.

A divorce, then, in Bantu Africa is not set in motion by any process comparable to the consultation of a solicitor for advice on the question whether a spouse's grievance is of a nature to allow him or her to be released from the marriage. It starts most commonly with a woman running home to her own family after a quarrel. Since it is taken for granted that she could not go anywhere else, her husband knows where she is, and should go after her, taking with him appropriate gifts in placation and in token of respect for her family. Ideally the wife's complaint should be discussed and her family should seek to reconcile them, sometimes adjudicating that the husband should make her some compensation. It is as much their moral obligation to persuade

the wife to go back as it is the husband's to come and fetch
her. This may happen more than once. If the wife refuses
(which is on the whole unlikely unless she has a lover), or the
husband neglects to come for her, the marriage may
effectively lapse. If it has been concluded by payment of
bridewealth in a patrilineal society, this is separation without divorce, since, as has been shown, the bridewealth
irrevocably fixes the status of a woman's children. In a matrilineal society, even where a cattle payment is made, there is
no significance in the distinction unless dispute arises about
repayment.

It is a historical accident that the most detailed studies of
divorce and the reasons held to justify it have been made
among matrilineal peoples. Much of this work was done
under the auspices of the Rhodes–Livingstone Institute,
which was founded to promote study of the effects of rapid
industrialization in the three Central African territories, and
in fact sponsored research mainly in what are now Zambia
and Malawi. As it happens, most of the peoples of those
countries are matrilineal; a comparable institution further
south would have found itself dealing with patrilineal
peoples. Such statistics as have been collected, there and
elsewhere, confirm the generally accepted view that there is
more divorce in matrilineal societies; but where records
going back in time have been obtained, they do not confirm
another widely held view – that marriage is becoming more
unstable in the degeneracy of modern times.

Ideas about the circumstances which justify a divorce are
not uniform throughout the area, and Native (now called
Local) Courts do not all take the same line on every point.
Thus Colson can write of the Plateau Tonga in Zambia: 'If
a husband goes off and does not return, no woman would
consider it necessary to go to the court for a divorce before
marrying another man.'[5] Of course her kin would return
whatever marriage payments they had received. Since it is
considered to be a woman's right to bear as many children as

5. E. Colson, *Marriage and the Family among the Plateau Tonga*,
1958, p. 162.

she can, and the women do not themselves regard this as a hardship, Tonga courts are disposed to release a woman whose husband is away for a long time, is impotent, or is prevented from cohabiting with her by some disease. But Ngoni courts in Zambia will not let a woman divorce an absentee unless he has been away without writing home for four years and they need to be convinced that she has tried to trace him; if he is impotent or has a contagious disease, they hold it to be his wife's responsibility to find medicines to cure him; and if he is sent to prison on a long sentence, they take the view that this was not his choice and his wife should wait for him. This greater strictness may be ascribed to the patrilineal tradition of the Ngoni, or possibly to the greater influence over them of Christian missions. Among the Lozi, who trace kinship at choice through either parent but marry with a bridewealth of three cattle, the 'prime minister's' court granted a divorce to a woman whose husband had been away for three years, although he sent her many gifts; the judge's comment was, 'This woman did not marry a blanket.' This case was recorded in 1947; the other data given were obtained in 1949. In the latter year the Malawian courts were endlessly occupied with demands for such divorces. Sometimes an absentee husband would have been sent for by his kin with the news that his wife had a lover; he would come home to collect damages for adultery but would agree to divorce. Tonga husbands, on the other hand, maintain through thick and thin that they want their wives back, in part because the courts regard it as reprehensible to demand divorce, and impose a fine on the party who does so. The Malawian courts usually fined a woman who sought divorce, the presumption being that she had committed adultery and her lover would pay.

What, then, are the reasons that are held to justify a woman in seeking a divorce? Essentially there are two, and they will be found in many other parts of the world than Central Africa: that her husband does not support her in those matters where she is dependent on him, viz. housing and clothing, and that he exceeds recognized limits in the exercise of his acknowledged right to beat her. An absentee husband can often meet his obligation to support his wife by sending her money; indeed, in many parts of rural Africa, a husband has to leave his wife for this very purpose.

Most accounts of African peoples agree that it is far more common for women to seek divorce than for men, but if a man does want to repudiate his wife he is on the whole not required to give specific justification; of course, if he does, his action is likely to follow on quarrels which third parties have done their best to reconcile. Nothing can prevent a man from turning his wife out; argument begins when he asks for his bridewealth back. According to some accounts he would be justified if she was a bad cook, particularly if she consistently failed to flavour the near-tasteless carbohydrate food that is the staple of so many African diets with what the books always call a 'relish'; or if she was repeatedly unfaithful; or repeatedly disobedient, especially in leaving home without his permission; or quarrelled with a co-wife whom he preferred. A husband might send away a wife who did not bear him children; in southern Africa her family would have the obligation to give him a sister of the barren wife, so a divorce would not be necessary.

Many accounts say baldly that 'witchcraft is a ground for divorce', but do not say what happens in actual cases. The laws of all former colonies, which have not been repealed, although it is possible that they are disregarded, make the imputation of witchcraft, not witchcraft itself, a crime; so that for a man to seek divorce on such a ground in a court would be impossible. It would be more realistic to say that public opinion would be on his side if he repudiated a wife who had been convicted of witchcraft—that is to say, in effect, accused with the acquiescence of public opinion; there is rarely unanimous agreement on the identification of a witch. Only two writers have given us any firm evidence on this point. One is the lawyer J. R. Crawford, who has examined a large number of cases in Rhodesia.[6] He found that some husbands said, 'I cannot live with a witch'; and one can

6. J. R. Crawford, *Witchcraft and Sorcery in Rhodesia*, 1967.

well believe that a man would take that line if, as often happened, his wife was held to be guilty of bewitching the child of a co-wife. But some husbands refused to believe the accusation. The other writer is the anthropologist Esther Goody; she found among the Gonja in northern Ghana a number of women who had been accused of witchcraft and driven away from their homes. But one was visited by her husband and several re-married. Witchcraft may be a 'ground for divorce', but it is not in fact a 'disqualification for marriage'. Some people like to have a witch on their side, and others don't believe she is one.

People who seek to compare the frequency of divorce in different societies – or even in different African societies, in itself quite a complex problem – invite the question 'What exactly do you mean?'. It is possible to find, as Fortes did with the Tallensi, a population where many men have been divorced half a dozen times and the majority of women at least once. But on inquiry it may prove, as it did with the Tallensi, that most of these divorces concern the earliest days of marriage – in the Tallensi case, before bridewealth arrangements have been completed. At this stage, a man gets rid of his wife either by making her life a misery, or by showing no sign of wanting to produce the marriage cattle, so that her guardian takes her away. A woman just runs away. Some of these unions only last a few weeks; they start with an elopement, but the couple repent before the youth has even approached the girl's parents. Tallensi call them 'marriages', and very likely the partners do not regard them as mere experiments, though that is how the anthropologist describes them. It may be a scholastic question whether the dissolution of a union that has not been finally legalized is to be called a divorce. The interesting fact is that in the societies where the records show divorces to be most frequent, the great majority happen in the early days of marriage and before the birth of children. If one accepts the view of many African societies that a marriage has not really come into being until a child is born and the couple are living in their own house – which may not be until even later – the number of divorces to be recorded as such falls sharply. The point has been made in a slightly different way by Esther Goody, who writes in her study of the Gonja: 'Frequent divorce during the early years of marriage, particularly before the birth of children, is consistent with high overall jural and conjugal stability of marriage'.[7]

Esther Goody's account of the Gonja, however, is not confined to the re-statement of a fact that has been noticed by others. She considers what happens to women whose marriages end in different ways and at different periods of their life. There is very little formal divorce in Gonja, since this is one of the societies in which a person derives his status from his actual father, no matter what was that man's legal relation to his mother. Marriage can be described as a domestic union in which childbearing is incidental, whereas the reverse would be truer of patrilineal people marrying with bridewealth. It lasts, therefore, as long as the couple are living together, and can be ended by a separation which may not originally have been intended as a final break. Since there is no bridewealth to be paid, a woman who has returned to her own kin becomes available for marriage as soon as she is inclined, and most of those who are of childbearing age find second husbands within a year or two. Widows are not inherited; on the contrary, a widow may not marry a kinsman of her husband. Older women, therefore, may anticipate widowhood by 'retiring from marriage', as it has been put, and going to live with a brother. So far from losing status by such a move, an elderly woman is not expected to be subordinate to him as she was to her husband; and his obligation to support her is recognized. She may move because of the belief that a sick woman can only find medicines among her own kin, or because she has been accused of witchcraft.

Gonja kinship structure is exceptional in the context of other societies described in this book. This account of it is given because it deals more fully than any other with the *different* occasions for the ending of marriage that arise at

7. E. Goody, in *Marriage in Tribal Societies*, ed. M. Fortes, 1962, p. 22.

different times of life. One way in which, to judge from
other accounts, the Gonja are exceptional is that the chances
that a marriage will last are apparently not increased by the
birth of children. All other writers agree that in patrilineal
African societies the birth of children who are kin to both
groups of affines brings them, as well as the parents themselves, into a closer and more friendly relationship, in which
the general interest in maintaining the marriage is enhanced.
Although divorce is more frequent in matrilineal societies,
they too believe that a marriage is firmly established when
children are born; it is then, and not before, that they
think it safe to let a woman be taken away from the protection of her kin.

Muslim Divorce

The ease of divorce in Muslim countries – one of those 'facts
that everybody knows' – is substantiated by recorded cases
from a number of them. For example Cunnison[8] calculated from a small sample that about 55 per cent of marriages contracted among a tribe of Baggara Arabs in the
Sudan end in divorce; and Judith Djamour,[9] using official
records, found that divorce rates (the proportion of divorces
to marriages in a given year) ranged from 41 to 61 per cent
in Java, while the Malay state of Perlis in 1952 had a rate of
92.7 per cent and most of the rest of Malaya over 50 per
cent, that for Malays in Singapore being 55.7 per cent in
1949.

We must remember that Islam is the religion and law of a
literate culture. Its holy book, the Koran, dates from the
seventh century, and the treatises on which its law is still
based today from the eighth. Commentaries, precedents, in-
terpretations to meet new circumstances have been accumulating ever since. From the earliest times the Muslim rulers
have appointed legal officials called Kadis (or Kathis or Al-

8. I. G. Cunnison, *Baggara Arabs*, 1966, p. 90.
9. J. Djamour, *Malay Kinship and Marriage in Singapore*, 1959, pp.
132-7.

calai, or many other alternatives depending on the local
language). Under colonial rules their numbers were increased,
they were required to keep records, and the laws they were
to administer were modified. Where marriage was concerned, the changes made were intended to improve the
position of the wife.

Islam today is the religion of societies ranging from
nomad herdsmen in Africa to wholly monetized city populations in Pakistan, Malaya and Java. Until the establishment of British rule the Fulani in Nigeria were dealing with
matrimonial disputes as quarrels between lineages, to be
arbitrated by their political heads, and sometimes they do today. The most important issue for them is the return of a runaway wife or the repayment of bridewealth; and bridewealth itself is a matter of African custom and not of Islamic
law. The Somali on the other hand, equally nomad and
equally remote from the urban setting to which the Kadis
belong, reckon that a divorce is not recognized, that is a
woman is not free to re-marry, unless the Kadi has issued a
document to that effect. Among the Muslim societies where
anthropologists have made intensive studies, the extreme of
sophistication is represented by Singapore, where Kadis
have been required for the past sixty years to register marriages and divorces, and where 150 divorce cases brought
during two years before a special court for matrimonial
affairs set up in 1958 were recorded fully enough to provide material for a book on the subject.

The basic rule in Muslim marriage is that a husband can
divorce his wife at will without giving a reason. He has only
to say: 'I divorce you'. Most accounts say the words must be
spoken before witnesses, but this seems not to be so in Singapore, perhaps because the requirement to register the repudiation is held to be equivalent. It takes effect from that
moment, but the woman may not re-marry for 100 days and
should spend that time in seclusion in her husband's home;
the delay is imposed in case she should prove to be pregnant
by him. During this time he may revoke the divorce, and
possibly people urge him to do so; in Singapore this is held to

be the Kadis' function. But once he has said 'I divorce you' three times – and he may do this in one breath – the divorce is irrevocable. Or rather, it cannot be cancelled unless in the meantime the woman has married another man and this man is willing to divorce her. Some people arrange for this purpose a formal marriage to be instantly dissolved, but Islam requires that any marriage which is duly solemnized should be consummated. Moreover, the cost of the new marriage and divorce must be borne by the first husband. Singapore Malays hesitate for other reasons to pronounce the triple repudiation; they believe that most husbands regret it and that this afflicts them with a special kind of madness. This might be added to our evidence that most people regard lasting marriage as an ideal; but of course it is possible for a revocable divorce to become final, particularly if the woman wants her freedom.

Muslim women cannot divorce their husbands in this cavalier manner, nor are there any specific grounds which are held to entitle them to release from a marriage. But they have ways of obtaining it, some provided by law and some not.

The nomad Fulani, although they purport to follow Islamic principles, are far from orthodox. They do allow a woman to repudiate her husband, and they do not allow a man to dismiss his wife with the Muslim formula of divorce. Divorce crystallizes out of separation as it commonly does among their pagan neighbours, and since there is no question among them of distant journeys to work for wages, it is the wife who creates the separation. She has to 'run away' in the sense of leaving home without being noticed. She may go back to her own family and appeal to the local chief to dissolve the marriage; this he generally does, since otherwise she is likely to adopt the alternative of escaping 'outside the jurisdiction' with some young man she has met at the market. A man divorces his wife by swearing a repudiation in the presence of the chief; he need give no reason, and she has no appeal, but since she must first have left him, he may have to treat her badly with the aim of making her do so. He proclaims the repudiation by removing the rope for tethering cattle that was fixed in place when she and her husband first acquired their independent household.

Derek Stenning, whose account of the Fulani[10] I am using, tells us that for a man the major reason to dissolve a marriage is that his wife does not bear children; Fulani do not know that this may happen because the husband is sterile. For a woman it is that her husband has not enough cattle to provide her and her children with enough milk. But couples quarrel, as they do anywhere. A man may give as reasons why he divorced his wife that she was disobedient, disgraced him by stealing goods in the market or was caught in adultery; a woman may complain that her husband went visiting and stayed away too long, pitched camp in places where she had too far to go for water or to market, or, more standard grievances, favoured another wife or was mean in buying her clothes.

Muslim women in Singapore have more ways of getting out of marriage than the standard description of Muslim divorce procedure would suggest. One that is not actually provided for by the law consists of putting it on record, at the time when the marriage is registered, that if the husband fails in certain respects he shall be held to have repudiated his wife (not irrevocably). The stipulations are intended to secure for her the minimum expected from a husband: that he should support his wife and should not subject her to physical cruelty (i.e. not beat her too much). Such an agreement generally stipulates (in effect) that she shall be free if he fails to maintain her for three months; there is room for plenty of argument about what 'support' amounts to. Some such agreements also make gambling a ground for this kind of automatic divorce.

A wife can also redeem or buy herself off; this consists more often in abandoning claims to unpaid marriage payments or to maintenance than in raising money herself. A new situation has arisen in Singapore since reforming authorities stipulated that a wife cannot be divorced without her consent, ensured by the requirement that both parties must sign the application to have a divorce registered. A

10. D. Stenning, *Savannah Nomads*, 1959.

wife who has no objection to the divorce can, by refusing to sign, blackmail her husband into making whatever property settlement she likes. The most striking case in Judith Djamour's records concerned a woman who maintained that she had given her husband no reason to divorce her, but who eventually agreed on condition that *all* the household goods (to which she had no right in law) were made over to her. The husband begged to keep his camera and tape-recorder, but she had already sold them for money to live on after he left her.

There is no denying, then, that Islamic law makes divorce easy and that many couples take advantage of this. It is probably as true of these divorces as of others where close observation has been made that many couples separate during the early years of arranged marriages. To have been divorced brings little discredit to a Muslim woman, and in her second marriage she is free to make her own choice.

This is true of Muslim societies which have been observed in many parts of the world. Yet there are some in which men do not avail themselves of the opportunities that Islam gives them. As will readily be imagined, these are the peoples who are wedded to the notion of honour. For some, to be placed in a situation where one has to divorce a wife is an occasion of great shame. Among the Pathans in Swat it would be assumed that the wife had been unfaithful with a man whom the husband did not dare to challenge. To divorce a wife over whom one is supposed to have absolute authority is, as Barth[11] puts it, to admit defeat.

Of another turbulent people, the nomad Bakhtiari of the mountains of Iran, an instance is recorded in which homicide was preferred to divorce. A woman whose husband persistently ill-treated her begged her father to let her divorce him, something that could only have been effected in practice by forcibly removing her and keeping her from her husband. The father preferred to kill the husband, and was generally held to have acted in an honourable manner.[12]

Anthropologists began to discuss the stability of marriage

11. F. Barth, *Political Leadership among Swat Pathans*, 1959, p. 40.
12. Information from Mr David Brooks.

in the context of bridewealth; the subject arose more or less incidentally in the course of their attempts to persuade European authorities that the institution of marriage with cattle payment was not a form of slave-trading. It is a good thing, we said; it is hard to break up a marriage if the bridewealth has to be returned, and the higher the bridewealth the harder it is. Evans-Pritchard was the first to argue that the more intangible consequences of the contact between affines and their common interest in the children of a family were the real support of marriage. Then Gluckman maintained that it was the other circumstances making marriage stable which led men to pay a high bridewealth.

Why is divorce common among Baggara Arab herdsmen and rare among Nilotic Nuer herdsmen? Why does a Pathan's honour preclude him from divorcing his wife when a Humr of the equally turbulent Baggara has no hesitation in doing so? A social anthropologist should look for the answer in differences in social structure; among these we must certainly take into account religious beliefs, which, some anthropologists would say, reflect social structure.

CHAPTER 12

MODERN TIMES

EXCEPT where I have expressly made the contrary clear, the rules and customs that I have described are still being followed by large numbers of people, despite the many changes that the penetration of western techniques and ideas has brought to the rest of the world. The first examples that I gave illustrated circumstances in which rules that were recognized in the past had been abandoned; they were meant to show what is actually the significance of expecting a couple who mean to found a family to make a public contract in a form that society prescribes. But for the most part the country people of the Third World – and they are still the great majority – cling to their traditional ideas of what a marriage should be and how it should be made legal, even after many other aspects of their life have been profoundly changed. Take the Nuer as an example. After the Sudan became independent, there was a rebellion of the southern peoples, which was suppressed with great severity; and it seems that they have lost many cattle, since nowadays, I believe, they flock into Khartoum to look for work. I am prepared to bet that they still marry with a cash equivalent of bridewealth and that the payment still has the same consequences. My reason for saying this is that the southern Bantu, who have depended for a century or more on wage-earnings to supplement what their farms produce, still maintain the same system of marriage law.

What has changed is the relationship between the couple and their kin. A marriage alliance is no longer such an important way of pursuing one's ambitions, though sometimes it may still be important. Sons can usually do much more to help their fathers by finding work away from home than by working the family farm under father's eye – that is, if they are dutiful and want to help their fathers. If they want to cut loose from the older generation altogether, who can stop them? If a man earns his own bridewealth, who is to say what girl he must marry? Not everyone does assert independence in this way, but it is a trend; it is a way of approaching marriage and its relation to kinship that was not practicable in earlier circumstances.

New Economic Conditions

What has created the new possibilities? In a very broad way, one can say, partly new economic conditions and partly new ideas. The new economic conditions exist everywhere; the new ideas have been much more influential in the East than they have in Africa. The easiest way to sum up the new economic conditions is to call what has happened the introduction of a money economy. Purists may find fault with this way of putting it. They can argue, and they have, that even if African societies did not have what we generally mean by money – some kind of token that you can exchange for anything you want to buy – many of them had objects of one kind or another that they used for particular types of exchange. Some economist-anthropologists even talk like this of cattle used as bridewealth. A stronger and more obvious objection is that money has been in use in the East for longer than it has in many parts of Europe. But the all-pervading effects of the money economy have only begun to be felt in these parts of the world – and indeed in some parts of rural England – in quite recent times.

In a thorough-going cash economy everyone has a money income, and nearly everyone gets his income by working for an employer. When we talk of a 'family business' we do not mean one in which all the personnel are kin, though that is what it would have meant in China or Japan; we just mean one in which brothers and cousins hold most of the shares. In an economy of this kind everyone looks in a different direction to make his way in life. Brothers enter different occupations from one another and from their fathers, and everyone looks to a source outside the extended family. What holds it together now is sentiment rather than necessity, and sentiment is weaker than necessity in restraining individual interests.

In Africa today nobody can do without earning some money, but the people who depend wholly on a money income are still a minority – civil servants, university teachers, politicians and the like. Some still get their cash income from the family farm, but for employment, and above all salaried employment, it is all but essential to live in a town. In the older parts of some West African towns there are still 'family compounds' built round square courtyards, with a separate section for each component family. But modern authorities do not provide this kind of housing, and even the well paid who can build their own houses do not usually plan them on such a scale. So individual families must live separately, and even if brothers move to town they are not likely to be able to find housing where they can be neighbours. The typical urban family in Africa, then, is one dependent wholly on an income earned from an employer right outside the range of kinship, and living with neighbours of similar income and social class but not necessarily related to it even remotely. When people can choose where to live they may prefer to live conveniently near their place of work rather than with close kin.

A striking illustration of what moving to town could imply for family life is provided by the arrangements that were made to re-settle the families displaced by the damming of the Volta River in Ghana, which has created the largest man-made lake in the world. These people were settled, in fact, in other villages, but housing was provided by the government, as it is more often in town. The building had to be done in a hurry, and it was eventually decided to give each family a 'core house' of *one room* and leave them to build on as many additions as they needed. Of the many people who complained of the houses one said he had a household of twenty-two.

It is fundamentally, however, the increasing dependence

on cash incomes that loosens family bonds. A comment that has been made on Chinese families in Singapore is that if the family income depends on a business it is in the interest of the sons to stay at home, and their wives must expect to live under the mother-in-law's authority as all wives did in the old days. Even if the business is a big one of modern type, sons with an eye to their share in control must please their fathers, if their fathers hold to traditional family ideas. But these cases are coming to be exceptional.

The opposite effect of new opportunities is described in the life-story of a Pakistani sociologist which is contributed to a number of essays dealing with changes in family life in Asia.[1] His father lived in the village home of his ancestors, with a widowed sister who depended on him. The brother had seven children, the sister eight. The father held up to his children the ideal of a Hindu joint family in a neighbouring district which consisted of forty members and organized its own highly successful school. He himself was an inspector of schools, and provided for the education of his children and nephews by taking them with him to the centres where he was posted, but he could not be persuaded to move permanently to a small town with a college. One by one the younger generation moved away as they found employment, not only because the work was in town but because they wanted to educate their children. When the story was written the writer and four brothers were living in Dacca, but not in the same house, nor did they expect married children to live with them.

I have emphasized the new sources of money income, and, for the fortunate, of advancement, which pull the members of extended families in different directions and often make it necessary for them to live in different places. But of course this is not simply a matter of reluctant acceptance of necessity. Professor Karim, the writer just quoted, gives reasons why he and his brothers prefer to live in the capital of East Pakistan. One is that in the village one cannot keep out of

1. A. K. Nazmul Karim, 'Changing Patterns of an East Pakistan Family', in *Women in the New Asia*, ed. Barbara E. Ward, 1963.

local politics. 'In an urban set-up, where relationships are more impersonal, we would be able to lead a more peaceful life.' The other is the greater freedom for women in town life. This is part and parcel of the independence of the nuclear family, in which the wife is mistress of her household from the beginning; town life may make this convenient or necessary, but those who desire it realize that it is impossible in the country.

'Those who desire it' are, of course, those with 'modern' ideas; and it is not much use for a woman to have such ideas unless her husband has them too. The rebellious wives of old-fashioned husbands have only the limited types of recourse that they had in the old days; men say everywhere that women in these days are more disobedient and less faithful than they used to be. Anthropologists who have taken records doubt this; it is what men always say.

New Ideologies

So we come to the question of the influence of new ideas. These ideas have come in the first place from Western-type education, and so they have affected first and most profoundly that section of the populations of the Third World who have been most 'exposed to' such education and as a result are qualified for the best paid and most sought-after jobs. This is the class in the newly independent states that is often called 'the new élite'.

These are the people whose incomes are envied and their style of life admired even by those who cannot hope to emulate it – the pace-setters for the community. The ideas have originally come to them from different sources, though once they can read with ease they cease to be passive receivers of what their teachers give them. At the present time a potent source is life as students in western countries (it would be interesting to know what they learn about family life in Moscow). For British territories in Africa the first source of new standards was missionary endeavour. The missionary ideal of lifelong monogamous marriage has never made a deep impression in Africa, though of course there are African Christians who accept and adhere to it. But one of the expressions of nationalist feeling in Africa has been to reassert the value of institutions that Europeans condemned, and if the African élite are themselves normally monogamous, they do not make the reform of African marriage in general one of their aims. The French tolerated rather than encouraged Christian missions, but their method of inculcating their own ideas of social relationships was to offer a higher status, with exemption from certain disabilities, to people who lived in accordance with French marriage and family law. Not many people applied for this higher status, but its existence, and the domination of French culture, no doubt had its effect. One would probably find that the French-speaking new élite differ little in style of life from their English-speaking neighbours.

In other parts of the world the story has been different. Both in India and in Singapore, for different reasons, marriage laws have been passed which, if they were known to and made use of by the majority of the population, would greatly change the nature of marital relationships. In neither case has the influence of Christianity been responsible, except in so far as one must recognize that ideas originating in western Europe must all bear some marks of the general Christian ambience in which they grew. Of course Christian missions have worked in both these countries, but they have always found it harder to make headway among peoples of literate culture, with their own professional expounders of traditional values, than among non-literate peoples. And it has never been assumed by those in authority, as it was quite widely in British territories in Africa, that to impart Christianity was an essential part of the 'civilizing' process.

The first officials of the East India Company were not particularly interested in the improvement of Indian life or morals. But with the beginning of the nineteenth century came a succession of governors inspired by Whig ideas in politics and Evangelical Christianity in morals. They were most interested in the reform of administration and revenue collection, but they were also concerned with the status of women, and this had come to be a matter of concern to a small number of Indians also; the most famous of these was Ram Mohun Roy, who in 1816 – long before the Indian government had adopted an education policy – founded a college to give education on modern lines. Ram Mohun Roy and his friends campaigned against *sati*, and although they thought it was premature to try to abolish it by legislation, they did not oppose a law which was passed to forbid it in 1829. This was followed in 1856 by a Widows Remarriage Act, which of course could do no more than say that the British authorities would recognize the second marriage of a widow as legal. In 1872 a law provided that persons who wished to marry outside the limits set by caste could make civil marriages, but only if they declared that they were not adherents of any religion. After India became independent a Hindu Marriage Code was enacted which, like its counterparts in other states with reforming nationalist leaders, recognizes only monogamous marriage as legal.

Singapore has been subject to influence from two directions. British authorities were concerned particularly with the welfare of women and children, and one of the measures they introduced was to raise the status of secondary wives. Such women by Chinese custom had a definitely inferior status, and were usually the social inferiors of the husband and his first wife; on the other hand their relationship to him was publicly recognized and they were often expected to live in his house, though they did not always do so. The Chinese distinguished them clearly from 'kept women'. Colonial legislators found that they could not make a clear distinction between the two classes of wife and pronounced that Chinese marriage was polygamous, with the consequence that all wives were now entitled to a share in the property of a husband who died intestate. Claims on this basis are sometimes made by women who, in Chinese eyes, are definitely no more than mistresses. Colonial legislation also gave married women the right to hold property of their own. It provided for the registration of marriages, on the basis of which claims could be brought.

But overseas Chinese have also been influenced by what

goes on in China, and there two revolutionary governments have sought to modernize marriage and the family. The Kuomintang introduced a civil code in 1931 and the Communist regime another, not very different, in 1950. Both aimed at the emancipation of women, and so prescribed monogamy and free choice in marriage. The Singapore People's Action Party, which came into power with self-government, at once introduced a Women's Charter, which did not recognize any form of secondary marriage and required that all marriages be registered.

Other nations which have sought to reshape marriage and the family by legislation are Turkey, where Mustafa Kemal introduced a whole civil code based on that of Switzerland after his revolution in 1922, and Japan, where a new civil code was enacted in 1947.

It can safely be said that these laws imposed by central governments are effective only among a small minority of most populations. The existence of the Hindu Marriage Code does not affect the truth of what is said in earlier chapters of this book about village India. The new codes are inspired by ideals, certainly; but new ideals by themselves make little headway unless circumstances change so as to give them practical advantages over the old ones. The practical disadvantages of polygyny are similar to those of the extended family: houses are designed for one family, and not for more, and the essence of the polygynous household is that each mother with her children has her own separate quarters. The other disadvantage of polygyny is its cost to a husband who no longer works a farm with wives and children, but must support them from an income earned in employment.

But there are still circumstances where polygyny has practical advantages, and some of these have arisen in modern times. Singapore provides examples of different reasons. According to Chinese tradition the duty of a wife to her mother-in-law was at least as important as her duty to her husband. So a married man who went to seek his fortune in Singapore would leave his wife behind, as a matter of principle as much as convenience. Then he would find he needed a domestic companion, and would marry a local woman who was known as his 'Singapore wife'. This woman would recognize that, if she and the 'China wife' should ever meet, she must accept the position of an inferior, but the likelihood was remote. Another occasion for taking a secondary wife arose when a man was going up in the world and his first wife was not as sophisticated as his new higher-class friends. Such a man would marry a second wife whom he liked to show off in public, and who, therefore, could not be expected to take the inferior position in the household that would traditionally have been hers. The stereotyped picture of this process assumes that she would be a night-club star, but she is just as likely to be an English-educated girl who has taken a course in one of the many popular 'charm schools'. Ann Wee, a former member of the Social Welfare Department in Singapore, from whom this information is taken, tells a story of a man who took such a girl as his second wife. After his first wife died she imperceptibly acquired the status of a senior wife, but he then married another, a hand in one of the factories he owned, who had no charm of manner or appearance, and spent most of his time with her. Neighbours commented that she was the type of woman he had been used to in his own family.[2]

'Mr Tan' was evidently less well educated than his presentable wife. But similar problems have arisen in Africa, where educated men find themselves playing the roles of politician or diplomat which require them to give and attend formal parties. In Europe it has been assumed for a long time now that wives are invited to such parties, and in the transition period before independence the protocol was established by Europeans seeking to initiate their African successors. Often the African women had no idea what was expected of them. Of course ambitious young men seek to marry western-educated girls; I remember the stern disapproval with which the headmistress of a girls' secondary

2. Ann Wee, 'Chinese Women of Singapore', in *Women in the New Asia,* ed. Barbara E. Ward, 1963.

school in Uganda (a good many years ago now) received a party of young men who visited her for this purpose. But these Ganda youths expected to live in a house modestly furnished in western style, eating meals together with their wives from a table covered with a cloth, and they simply wanted to marry girls accustomed to such surroundings. They did not have to face the problems of formal hospitality of European type that confront some African politicians and diplomats of today, nor to enter a world in which it is part of the role of a wife to take the lead on certain social occasions. Of course many African politicians' wives do this with great success, but they are found for the most part in the West African areas with a longer tradition of education and overseas travel. It has been reported particularly of the Congo that Africans attend social engagements accompanied by female partners who have been described as 'professional hostesses'. These in fact are found among the independent women of the cities who were officially categorized by the Belgians as 'free women' (*femmes libres*). Such women are not prostitutes in any strict sense. But they *are* women who prefer independence to marriage and maintain their independence by means of the presents they receive from lovers; they do not want to marry, and those Congolese men who still hold to the old-fashioned ideal of the quiet domestic wife do not want to marry them. The Chinese phrase, 'The domestic flower cannot attain the fragrance of the wild bloom', describes the Congolese attitude too, but a Congolese, if he were to *marry* more than one wife, would expect them all to be domestic flowers.

Independent Women

In the Congo, however, there are grades of *femmes libres*. Only the most successful become the companions of politicians. But there are also *femmes libres sérieuses*, a term which recalls the approving phrase *jeune fille sérieuse* applied in France to a good girl who moves from the role of dutiful daughter to that of dutiful wife. 'Serious free women' are those with some professional qualification which brings them an independent income, who simply prefer not to marry. They are not too serious to take lovers, but many have a permanent association with one man that would rank with the informally established marriages that have been described earlier.

We come back again to the solvent of so many of the ties that bind the members of a small-scale society together – the dependence of individuals on relationships outside the kin and neighbourhood group. To say that women are 'independent' means that they are dependent on an income that they earn for themselves and not on a share of their husbands'; but, as a consequence, they can, if they prefer it, be independent of marriage.

Yet the fact that a woman can earn an income for herself does not lead most of them to eschew marriage, and the significant question in a study of changing marriage relationships is where, and how far, this is regarded as a suitable activity for a wife. Different circumstances have made it possible, or necessary, in different places. In central Africa, where men are away from home for months or years at a time working for wages, women brew beer or sometimes make pots for sale to meet some of their cash needs. In western Africa, market trading has been women's main occupation for many generations. Nadel, in his description of Nupe Emirate in Nigeria between the wars, tells how the surplus produce of the family farm is sold by the wife, who gets a share of the price. From this she must buy salt and other flavourings for the family meal. She also buys the ingredients of delicacies which she makes and sells, and even her husband, if he wants these, must buy them from her. Some husbands borrow money from their wives to pay their taxes, and some women are the main support of their families.

With the coming of road and rail transport women can go further afield, and may be away from home for weeks or months at a time. It is assumed that in such travels women add to their earnings by prostitution. At first only barren women, who could be said to have failed as wives, went on these long journeys, but by 1935 more and more young women with children were among the long-distance traders. Their husbands deplored this but did not repudiate them when they came home; so in a sense it could be said that their activities were not destructive of family life. However, Nadel associated with the husbands' resentment the fact that in Nupe witches are always believed to be women, and that the head of the witches in any village is thought to be the real woman who has been appointed by the chief as head of the women traders.

According to the ideal of marriage propagated in Africa by European education, good husbands do not 'make their wives work'. This principle was enunciated with back-breaking work in the fields in mind, but it also embodies the ideal of the wife and mother 'whose place is the home'. Women who go with their husbands to the big employment centres have no such work to do, but they have sometimes found that it was not an unmixed advantage to be making no contribution to the joint household and be completely dependent on the husband's earnings. The husbands for their part have complained that their wives get into mischief with too little to do.

But among politicians, civil servants and professional people in the new states, it appears to be the rule that both husbands and wives have paid employment, and this as much in countries where women used to be secluded as in those where they moved about freely. This may be a response to those ideals of the emancipation of women which some Indian reformers have championed; but ideas usually need material circumstances to drive them home, and in this case the circumstances have been identical inside and outside Europe. The crucial factor has been the inflation, particularly during and after the Second World War, which made it impossible for many families to maintain a standard of living that they thought adequate unless both parents were earning. In Europe working-class wives had 'gone out to work' for a long time, but this was apt to be interpreted by critics higher up the income scale as evidence of the laziness, or some other defect of character, of their husbands.

In a collection of essays published a few years ago under the auspices of Unesco a number of writers, both men and women, discussed the new roles of women in different countries of Asia. Only Japan was not covered. One of the Burmese writers refers to 'the modern household where both the husband and wife have their own careers',[3] and most of the other contributors take this for granted; of course they would not have written these essays if they had not belonged to the highly educated minority.

This type of modern household is by no means taken for granted in Britain, and still less on the continent of Europe. One hears increases in juvenile delinquency blamed on mothers who work in factories and neglect their children. Mothers in social classes that have traditionally employed servants have the advantage in Asia; there are plenty of servants to look after their children. But one writer comments wryly that instead of the old-style mother-in-law problem there is now an amah (nanny) problem; this is something that was not unknown in Europe in an earlier generation.

Social change outside northern Europe and America is commonly seen as a process of catching up with the 'west', and in the field of industrialization this is a reasonable way to look at it. But in the context of marriage and family relationships it is important to realize that the 'modern' families of Africa and Asia are not following at a great distance in the footsteps of Europe. Sixty years ago wives in London were threatened with marital sanctions if they joined women's suffrage demonstrations. Fifty years ago French friends of mine were shocked when one of their number got engaged without seeking her parents' approval. Forty years ago men whose wives had professional qualifications equal to their own might much dislike the idea that these women should follow their professions, and thus prevent it although they could not actually forbid it. Mothers intervened in their

3. Ni Ni Gyi, 'Patterns of Social Change in a Burmese Family', in *Women in the New Asia*, ed. Barbara E. Ward, 1963, p. 147.

daughters' marriage choices, sometimes with a veto and
sometimes with presssure to accept the maternal choice;
again, though, children were not committed by their
parents. Champions of oppressed womanhood overseas have
often been satisfied with the status quo at home.

The Atomization of Kinship

The discussion of changes in marriage relationships has
turned into a discussion of the progress of feminism. This can
be justified in so far as the trend of change has been a movement away from that disposal of women by men which
has been one of my major themes. But I am not primarily
concerned with the status of women, or the justice and
degree of success of their claims to equality. Rather I am
seeking to show how in an economy based on large-scale production every member of a family tends, through employment, to become linked to the outside world in a
different direction. Family resources are no longer pooled,
and individuals who have not depended, except as children,
on family resources, sometimes see no reason to use their
own resources to support less fortunate kin. This is by no
means universal; in Yoruba country in Nigeria, for example,
the tradition has grown up that parents put one child
through a university and this one, son or daughter, should be
responsible for educating the other siblings. Professional
men seek posting away from home to be out of reach of the
constant demands of their kinsmen for help – but this is
precisely because they cannot turn a deaf ear. In the affluent
countries, public funds now provide for all needy persons,
not only those who have no kin. In the poorer ones there is
an unfilled gap where more distant kinsmen, even perhaps
sometimes aged parents, are neglected for the sake of the
constantly rising expectations of the nuclear family.

So one aspect of the family ideal of western moralists is
winning the day: the conception of the nuclear family in
which the father is wholly committed to one woman and her
children, and both parents have commitments to their chil-

dren that are prior to any others. Freedom of choice in marriage, freedom from subordination of the new household to the older generation, are coming to be taken for granted as principles, and the latter is being forced by circumstances. Divorce has been made easy where it was difficult before – something that is not in everyone's eyes a part of the ideal.

But on the heels of changes that have been hailed as reforms come lamentations over the atomization of modern society and, worse still, the shortcomings of the atom itself (if that is what the nuclear family is). 'The family with its tawdry secrets' is a phrase that will soon find its way into dictionaries of quotations. The emphasis has shifted from claims on behalf of women to claims on behalf of children; at least the remedies suggested by Edmund Leach lie in the collective rearing of children rather than in changes in the relationship of husband and wife. Like many others who find the nuclear family stifling, he offers the kibbutz as an alternative; one might perhaps add the hippy colony.

But it is not easy to picture a contemporary society consisting entirely of kibbutzim, let alone hippy colonies. The kibbutz is an enclave in a state where most people earn their living in individual contracts of employment. The most thorough-going collectivist governments have not sought to abolish the family, even though they may have made it easier to break the bonds of marriage, and even when they have encouraged children to denounce their parents for political offences. And since the hippy colony is for people who contract out of society as at present organized, and reject as many of its material aspects as they can while still keeping alive, it is not an example for the many to whom the affluent society appeals.

Those who have been able to benefit from the inventions that save burdensome labour, increase health, and create enjoyment are still too few, but it would be dangerous to assume that many people do not want them ('they were happier before'). They get them only in a world of specialization and employment outside the family, with the consequences for it that this chapter has described. It is disconcerting to find the family ideal that the non-European societies have so recently adopted being already rejected (though of course not widely). But it seems to be the price – if it is a price – of such material satisfactions as the twentieth century can give.

SUGGESTIONS FOR FURTHER READING

NOT all the books I have quoted have a great deal to say about marriage, although, since it is a basic human institution, every anthropologist has something to say about it. The books and articles I shall mention here, with the exception of some on India, deal with it from the point of view of social analysis, that is the dissection of a society into the groups of which its structure is formed. Many of them deal with topics mentioned in more than one chapter, so I am classifying them by continents and not by chapters. To begin with, however, I must mention two which discuss the general subject of marriage in relation to kinship. Of these a very large one is Lévi-Strauss, *Elementary Structures of Kinship* (English translation 1968), which every student ought to be able at least to talk about, and a very good small one is Robin Fox, *Kinship and Marriage* (1967), which inaugurated the Pelican Anthropology Library; it covers the subject of incest, which I have deliberately omitted on that account.

AFRICA

J. A. Barnes, *Marriage in a Changing Society* (1951). This is the first book to show how marriage as a means of legalizing paternity can lose importance when status ceases to depend on patrilineal descent.

E. M. Colson, *Marriage and the Family among the Plateau Tonga* (1958). A matrilineal society where cattle are paid at marriage.

M. Douglas, *The Lele of the Kasai* (1963). A system of polyandry.

E. E. Evans-Pritchard, *Kinship and Marriage among the Nuer* (1951, 2nd edn 1960). The first book to discuss systematically the significance of bridewealth for the paternity of children.

M. Fortes, *The Web of Kinship among the Tallensi* (1949). Particularly admirable for its account of domestic life.

M. Fortes, ed., *Marriage in Tribal Societies* (1962). Contains discussions (by G. Harris and J. La Fontaine) of reasons for choice in marriage alliances, and also reasons for preferring to have bride-wealth payments completed or left incomplete; also an essay by E. Goody on the incidence of divorce at different periods of a woman's life among the Gonja (northern Ghana).

M. Fortes, 'Time and Social Structure', in a collection of essays published under this title (1970). Describes the Ashanti system in which husbands and wives live in separate houses.

M. Gluckman, 'Kinship and Marriage among the Lozi of Northern Rhodesia and the Zulu of Natal', in *African Systems of Kinship and Marriage* (1950). Discusses the relation between different types of marriage payment and the stability of marriage.

B. Pauw, *The Second Generation* (1963). About an urban population in South Africa where many couples do not marry.

A. I. Richards, *Bemba Marriage and Present Economic Conditions* (1940). The most detailed study we have of marriage in a matrilineal society.

A. I. Richards, *Chisungu* (1956). An account of Bemba girls' puberty rites.

I. Schapera, *Married Life in an African Tribe* (1940). The tribe are Tswana, and modern changes are fully explored.

M. Wilson, *Rituals of Kinship among the Nyakyusa* (1957). Contains a detailed analysis of the symbolism of marriage ritual.

AMERICA

R. T. Smith, *The Negro Family in British Guiana* (1956). Explains why many Negro parents don't get married.

ARABS

A. Cohen, *Arab Border Villages in Israel* (1965).
I. G. Cunnison, *Baggara Arabs* (1966).
I. M. Lewis, *Marriage and the Family in Northern Somaliland* (1962).
E. Marx, *Bedouin of the Negev* (1967).

All these books discuss choices in marriage and the reasons given by Arabs for the marriage of parallel cousins.

ASIA

(a) General

The Unesco volume, *Women in the New Asia* (1963), edited by Barbara E. Ward, contains articles (not all by women) on the changing roles of women in different Asian countries. Japan is not covered. The most valuable articles are the editor's introduction, one on Singapore by Ann Wee, two on India by S. C. Dube and A. K. Nazmul Karim, and a brief history of reforming movements in India by Romilla Tharpar.

(b) China and Singapore

J. Djamour, *Malay Kinship and Marriage in Singapore* (1959).

J. Djamour, *The Muslim Matrimonial Court in Singapore* (1966).

M. Freedman, 'Colonial Law and Chinese Society', in *Journal of the Royal Anthropological Institute* (1950).

M. Freedman, *Chinese Lineage and Society* (1966).

M. Freedman, *Rites and Duties* (1967).

The two last mentioned discuss the way in which each new marriage both adds to a family and eventually disrupts it, the first from the secular, the second from the ritual, point of view.

Ann Wee, 'Chinese Women of Singapore', in *Women in the New Asia*, ed. Barbara E. Ward (1963).

(c) India and Ceylon

G. D. Berreman, *Hindus of the Himalayas* (1963). Contains a number of marriage songs in addition to those I have quoted.

S. C. Dube, 'Men's and Women's Roles in India', in *Women in the New Asia*, ed. Barbara E. Ward (1963).

Z. Eglar, *A Punjabi Village in Pakistan* (1960). By a pupil of Margaret Mead. Gives interesting descriptions but does not make principles clear.

E. K. Gough, 'Female Initiation Rites on the Malabar Coast', in *Journal of the Royal Anthropological Institute* (1955). Discusses the 'mock marriage' rituals of some south Indian societies.

T. N. Madan, *Family and Kinship* (1965). On a Hindu population in Kashmir.

A. K. Nazmul Karim, 'Changing Patterns of an East Pakistan Family', in *Women in the New Asia*, ed. Barbara E. Ward (1963).

M. N. Srinivas, *Religion and Society among the Coorgs of South India* (1952). Describes marriage procedures in an only partially sanskritized society.

R. Tharpar, 'The History of Female Emancipation in Southern Asia', in *Women in the New Asia*, ed. Barbara E. Ward (1963).

N. Yalman, *Under the Bo Tree* (1967). An excellent account of marriage in Ceylon.

N. Yalman, 'On the Purity of Women in the Castes of Ceylon and Malabar', in *Journal of the Royal Anthropological Institute* (1963), pp. 25–58. An alternative hypothesis on 'mock marriages'.

(d) Japan

R. P. Dore, *City Life in Japan* (1958). Part III is concerned with changes in marriage and family life.

AUSTRALIA

L. Hiatt, *Kinship and Conflict* (1965). How 'prescribed cross-cousin marriage' really works in practice.

THE MEDITERRANEAN

J. Campbell, *Honour, Family and Patronage* (1964). Honour among Greek shepherds.

J. Davis, 'Honour and Politics in Pisticci', in *Proceedings of the Royal Anthropological Institute* (1969).

J. Pitt-Rivers, ed., *Mediterranean Countrymen* (1963). Contains useful material on dowry.

THE PACIFIC

B. Malinowski, *The Sexual Life of Savages* (1929).

M. Mead, *Coming of Age in Samoa* (1928; Pelican, 1963). Some information about the value placed on virginity.

M. J. Meggitt, *The Lineage System of the Mae Enga* (1965).

M. Reay, *The Kuma* (1959).

Anthropologists in New Guinea have been less interested in marriage than have Africanists, but these last two books deal with it fairly extensively.

INDEX

MORE ABOUT PENGUINS
AND PELICANS

Penguinews, which appears every month, contains details
of all the new books issued by Penguins as they are
published. From time to time it is supplemented by
Penguins in Print, which is a complete list of all books
published by Penguins which are in print. (There are well
over three thousand of these.)

A specimen copy of *Penguinews* will be sent to you free on
request, and you can become a subscriber for the price of
the postage. For a year's issues (including the complete
lists) please send 30p if you live in the United Kingdom,
or 60p if you live elsewhere. Just write to Dept EP,
Penguin Books Ltd, Harmondsworth, Middlesex, enclosing
a cheque or postal order, and your name will be added to
the mailing list.

Note: *Penguinews* and *Penguins in Print* are not available in
the U.S.A. or Canada

Pelican Anthropology Library

Primitive Government   *Lucy Mair*

This summary of the way in which government is conducted without modern technical equipment throws much new light on the historical evolution of many of the institutions we have come to take for granted.

Kinship and Marriage   *Robin Fox*

This Pelican provides the first analysis of all the theories of kinship and marriage within a single framework of argument intelligible to the layman.

Taboo   *Franz Steiner*

'His book will be found to be of great value to anyone interested in the idea of taboo and to those who in the future tackle once more the problems it raises . . . it states in small compass, but with equal learning and wit, everything of any significance which has been written about taboo' – Professor E. E. Evans-Pritchard

Totemism*   *Claude Lévi-Strauss*

An excellent introduction to the structuralist approach to anthropology and to the thought of one of the most distinguished and interesting minds of our time.

Purity and Danger*   *Mary Douglas*

In this fascinating study Mary Douglas shows how the idea of contagion is at work in the weak points of every conceptual structure, and analyses the rituals through which its symbols of danger and power are contained.

Married Life in an African Tribe*   *Isaac Schapera*

Designed more for the general reader than the anthropologist, this famous study of the Kgatla of Bechuanaland describes the relations between the sexes in that community.

Ecstatic Religion   *I. M. Lewis*

States of spiritual exaltation are found in almost all known religions. *Ecstatic Religion* offers a sociological approach to this type of experience.

Not for sale in the U.S.A.